Cambridge Elements

Elements in Histories of Emotions and the Senses
edited by
Rob Boddice
Tampere University
Piroska Nagy
Université du Québec à Montréal (UQAM)
Mark Smith
University of South Carolina

MAKING SENSE OF KNOWLEDGE

Feminist Epistemologies in the Greek Birth Control Movement (1974–1986)

Evangelia (Lina) Chordaki
Princeton University

Shaftesbury Road, Cambridge CB2 8EA, United Kingdom

One Liberty Plaza, 20th Floor, New York, NY 10006, USA

477 Williamstown Road, Port Melbourne, VIC 3207, Australia

314–321, 3rd Floor, Plot 3, Splendor Forum, Jasola District Centre,
New Delhi – 110025, India

103 Penang Road, #05–06/07, Visioncrest Commercial, Singapore 238467

Cambridge University Press is part of Cambridge University Press & Assessment,
a department of the University of Cambridge.

We share the University's mission to contribute to society through the pursuit of
education, learning and research at the highest international levels of excellence.

www.cambridge.org
Information on this title: www.cambridge.org/9781009488464

DOI: 10.1017/9781009488433

© Evangelia (Lina) Chordaki 2025

This publication is in copyright. Subject to statutory exception and to the provisions
of relevant collective licensing agreements, no reproduction of any part may take
place without the written permission of Cambridge University Press & Assessment.

When citing this work, please include a reference to the DOI 10.1017/9781009488433

First published 2025

A catalogue record for this publication is available from the British Library

ISBN 978-1-009-48846-4 Hardback
ISBN 978-1-009-48845-7 Paperback
ISSN 2632-1068 (online)
ISSN 2632-105X (print)

Cambridge University Press & Assessment has no responsibility for the persistence
or accuracy of URLs for external or third-party internet websites referred to in this
publication and does not guarantee that any content on such websites is, or will remain,
accurate or appropriate.

For EU product safety concerns, contact us at Calle de José Abascal, 56, 1°, 28003
Madrid, Spain, or email eugpsr@cambridge.org

Making Sense of Knowledge

Feminist Epistemologies in the Greek Birth Control Movement (1974–1986)

Elements in Histories of Emotions and the Senses

DOI: 10.1017/9781009488433
First published online: June 2025

Evangelia (Lina) Chordaki
Princeton University
Author for correspondence: Evangelia (Lina) Chordaki, echorda@eie.gr

Abstract: What counts as knowledge, expertise, and theory? How are knowledge hierarchies connected to emotional and hierarchies of subjects? How does the division between emotion and reason shape our experiences? The Element addresses these questions by exploring the Greek feminist birth control movement (1974–1986), focusing on the production and circulation of knowledge, termed as *affective epistemologies of antimilima* (talking back). This concept reinterprets women's lived and embodied knowledge, emerging at the intersection of academia and social movements, as a form of resistance against established expertise. By drawing on feminist theorists like Donna Haraway and Sara Ahmed, the Element critically examines the relationship between scientific and experiential knowledge. This analysis reconfigures the interplay between rationality and emotion, providing a critique to the binary model of thought and suggesting new avenues for democratic knowledge, society, and citizenship. Historical tracing of these theories offers a counter-narrative to contemporary anti-gender, anti-intellectual, and far-right politics.

Keywords: gender, epistemology, emotion, abortion, expertise

© Evangelia (Lina) Chordaki 2025

ISBNs: 9781009488464 (HB), 9781009488457 (PB), 9781009488433 (OC)
ISSNs: 2632-1068 (online), 2632-105X (print)

Contents

Introduction: *Antimilima*   1

1 Situated Methodological Considerations   10

2 *Againstness*: Affective Economies and the Birth Control Debate   20

3 *Forness*: Sweaty Concepts and Women's Experiential Expertise   37

Conclusions: Making *Sense*   52

References   57

Introduction: *Antimilima*

February 1983, Athens (Greece). A moment of *antimilima*. The Autonomous Women's Movement Campaign, organizing under the title *The Right to Abortion-Contraception-Sexuality*, releases a document signed by 500 women who publicly declare that they have had abortions. This was one of the many acts of back speaking, answering, or talking back to the reality that 300,000–500,000 illegal abortions took place in Greece every year. The Greek word *antimilima* [αντιμιλη- (αντιμιλώ) –μα] refers to such acts. The prefix *anti* [αντί-] evokes the tension of contradiction and objection, opposition and rejection, reaction and replacement. The word also connotes impenitence, boldness, shamelessness, and self-assurance.

As a feminist concept, *Antimilima* can be traced back to bell hooks' notion of *talking back*. An act that includes premises, possibilities, limits, commitments, demands, and visions (1989). It poses questions and ensures that they resist stable answers. It produces and is produced by affective economies, bodies, emotions, and epistemologies. It maps their registration points through acts, discourses, fights, and struggles. It is the space and the absence of space – the *topos* and *utopia*. *Antimilima* is being, bonding, doing, and thinking, moving, and feeling. To talk back is to dare, disagree, confront, challenge, reclaim, recover, risk, and belong. As such, it creates a world in which acts of resistance are situated (see Haraway, 1988). *Antimilima* is world-knowing and world-making. Subjugated knowledges erupt and revolt as acts of resistance while operating as performative perforations. As Sara Ahmed argues, such acts of speaking out or speaking against imply a confrontation with established truths (2004, p.168), thus turning critical epistemologies into *antimilima* (Athanasiou, 2023).

This Element is an examination of the practices of knowledge production and circulation within the Greek feminist birth control movement during the era of the Democratic transition (1974–1986). It is a history of confronting institutional forms of knowledge and expertise and invading hostile intellectual and epistemic spaces (Puwar, 2004). The study focuses on how feminist activists transformed their experiences by reclaiming their relationship with knowledge while at the same time centralizing the crucial role of emotions as being understood within the specific historical and cultural context (see, indicatively, Reddy, 2000; Dixon, 2011; Rosenwein & Riccardo, 2018). This mobilization of experience is what I will call affective epistemology of antimilima. A history of how experiences of being feminists transformed knowledge production about birth control by critically renegotiating the binary of emotion versus reason.

As affective epistemologies of *antimilima*, these bodies of knowledge that are themselves *about* the body depict the crucial role of the geographical and epistemological peripheries, re-centering the collective localities of the gendered bodies that *feel* and *experience* without separating emotions and the senses (Boddice & Smith, 2020). This history of the relationship between affect, experience, and knowledge operates as a critique of and a response to parallel hierarchies established among emotions, subjects, and forms of knowledges, as well as the established division between reason and emotions (Ahmed, 2004, p. 3). Thus, body politics, politics of knowledge, and politics of emotions establish a feminist framework for the critical re-examination of the relationship between authoritative forms of knowledge –scientific knowledge and expertise– and epistemologies of *antimilima* – experiential knowledge and expertise (see, indicatively, Davies et al., 2019), "contesting the understanding of emotion as the unthought and that of the rational as the unemotional" (Ahmed, 2004, p. 170).

The Greek feminist birth control movement emerged during the twentieth century. From a global historical perspective, the twentieth century witnessed the contradictory emergence of both oppression and emancipation. Genocide, widespread migration, and refugee crises existed simultaneously with the recognition of human rights and struggles for women's emancipation. Different kinds of utopias were imagined and realized, though many devolved into dystopia (Liakos, 2022, p. 15).

Focusing on twentieth-century Greece and its historical and sociopolitical context, we notice the intertwining of Greek and global history, Greece's openness toward the different historical currents of the period (Liakos, 2022, p. 20), and the creation of a "unique fiery composition between the old and new, the local and transnational, the repetition and change" (Liakos, 2022, p. 23). As twentieth-century Greece has a long and complex history too large in scope for this project, I will now focus on the last decades – the era of the Democratic Transition (Metapolitefsi), after the fall of the dictatorial regime in 1974, to provide the historical context of the period in which the feminist birth control movement is situated.

The historical and political significance of the fall of the dictatorial regime is apparent in the analysis of Greek scholars, signifying the "collapse of the post-civil war political and governmental system" (Kostis, 2018, p. 792). It has also been characterized as a momentous historical period of significant change – a "breakthrough moment in the Greek political history of the second half of the 20th century" (Liakos, 2022, p. 409), "the Big Bang of contemporary Greece" (Liakos, 2022, p. 462), a "landmark in the contemporary Greek history"

(Pavlopoulos & Fitili, 2017), or a "chronotopos" (χρονοτόπος) (Avgeridis, Gazi, & Kornetis, 2015, p. 17).

During the Metapolitefsi period, democratic reformations changed the state's profile, transforming Greece from rural to urban in the 1960s. At the same time, the cultural changes of the 1970s included the transformation of social relationships and gender dynamics mass consumption, migration, mass tourism, the arts, the sexual revolution, and the contraceptive pill. Other major shifts included autonomy from the family, the creation of new social spaces, the visibility of nudity, the advent of leisure time, the emergence of subcultures and underground cultures, and the rise of negotiation and resistance (Liakos, 2022, pp. 411–14). Similarly, these decades undergo political and financial stability, intense politicization, the emergence of social and political movements, the visibility of different and/or new social groups that struggled for the abolition of oppression (Pavlopoulos & Fitili, 2017). At the same time, it has been argued that the 1960s and 1970s are characterized by specific characteristics that differentiate this period from the previous decades, including the crucial role of politicization in the many aspects of social life and within the whole region (Serdedakis, 2015, p. 108).

The set of reformations that lasted from 1975 to 1985 and included the decriminalization of abortion (1986) was enacted by the governments of both the right-wing party New Democracy (1974–1981) and the socialist Party PASOK (1981–1985) (Liakos, 2022, p. 425), with the former envisioning a "mediocre conservative-liberal democracy" (Kostis, 2018, p. 805) and the latter expressing a "movement against the political and economic Establishment" (Liakos, 2022, p. 425), which included "less privileged Greek citizens" (Kostis, 2018, p. 809). It is worth noting that these reformations were also part of the country's inclusion into the European Community (January 1, 1985), which was accompanied by "the political, economic and social modernization," the democratization, and the protection and promotion of civil rights (Rizas, 2017). Reform effected education, family law, gender and social relations, the welfare state, health, mental health, and human and political rights (Liakos, 2022, pp. 425–34).

Metapolitefsi and the fall of the dictatorial regime were therefore identified with the dynamic emergence of social and political movements (feminist, LGBT, anti-militarist, the ecological/antinuclear, social for peace), which "shaped the balances and priorities of this period" (Karamanolakis & Karpozilos, 2017). Here, the university's role was crucial. It ensured the necessary conditions for the politicization of the young generation, for whom *autonomy* was central to questioning the political and social establishment

(Karamanolakis & Karpozilos, 2017).[1] In fact, autonomy is significant to multiple movements, campaigns, and groups of the Metapolitefsi period that use the term in their slogans and names (i.e., Autonomous Women's Movement). An emphasis on autonomy also contributed to the appearance of autonomous publishing houses, as well as the sheer number of social movements at work. Thus, the Greek feminist (birth control) movement belongs to these "multiple cultures of Metapolitefsi" (Liakos, 2022, p. 441), embodying these aspects of its historical context.

The first organized efforts to improve women's lives in Greece took place in the middle of the nineteenth century, aiming to improve women's social position and access to education. The first women's associations and magazines focusing on women's participation in public life and elections did not emerge until the late nineteenth century (Varika, 2011 [1986]; Samiou 2013; 2012). Within the first decades of the twentieth century, there is a systematic presence of women's organizations and women's participation in the Communist Party, mainly focusing on their political rights, equity, working conditions, access to education, family, and motherhood. Between 1940 and 1974, several antifascist women's organizations and other unions emerged, which were later criminalized by the military Junta (Catalog, 2017).

The Polytechnic Uprising that took place in Athens in 1973 and the fall of the dictatorial regime shaped the Greek social and political sphere where feminist movements emerged.[2] During that period, many Greek women who lived abroad, mainly in Italy and France, and had participated in the European feminist movements of these countries returned to Greece. The ideological framework of European feminist movements therefore influenced the discourses and practices developed within the Greek birth control movement. Until 1986, when abortions were decriminalized, 300,000–500,000 illegal and unsafe abortions took place in Greece every year (Hestia, 1986; Avgi 1, 1986). Due to the lack of official statistics, the accurate number of illegal abortions remains unknown, and data regarding deaths or severe complications to women's health from unsafe abortions are not available. Within these decades, the use of contraception was significantly limited, while sex education programs were absent, and family planning services were limited and did not focus on women's needs. To that end, abortion was transformed into the primary contraceptive method for Greek women, while traditional (and inefficient) methods such as the withdrawal method remained popular.

---

[1] For the emergence and the role of "youth" as the actor of social change see Papadogiannis (2015).
[2] For the history of feminism in Greece, see indicatively: Xiridaki K. (2020); Avdela E., and Psarra A. (1985). Here I refer only to the feminist movements that emerged in the Greek public sphere in the second half of the twentieth century and especially to those related to birth control.

Thus, since its inception in 1976, the feminist movement has focused on the decriminalization of abortion and the need for circulating medical information about contraception. This dual aim of the feminist birth control movement soon showcased the differences among participating social groups.[3] On the one hand, autonomous feminist groups approached the decriminalization of abortion and the increase in availability of contraception by developing a feminist critique against the masculine character of the dominant science, focusing on self-organization, self-education, and self-determination of the female body. On the other hand, women's organizations and associations, primarily linked to political parties, discussed the issue in relation to family planning, and their demands focused on the institutional framework. Despite their various approaches, both groups coexisted in the Greek public arena, sometimes exchanging arguments, and often following completely different paths[4].

The emergence of the autonomous feminist movement for abortion and contraception is identified with the formation of the Movement for the Liberation of Women in 1976. Its first appearance was accompanied by its introductory brochure, which stated that abortion is not a contraceptive method and should be free and legal, even for underaged girls (Avdela et al., 1986, p. 9). In 1976, a successful public exhibition regarding contraceptive methods was organized by the Group of Sexuality of the Movement for the Liberation of Women, while at the same time, the Greek Association for Family Planning was established, and the Democratic Women's Movement started working on issues related to abortions (Movement, 1977; Avdela et al., 1986, pp. 10–11).

Abortions appeared in the Greek penal code for the first time in 1834, drafted by the Regency Council of Otto of Greece (LHP 1, 1835). More specifically,

---

[3] The use of the term "social group" is informed by Iris Marion Young's analysis. As she states, "A social group is a collective of persons differentiated from at least one other group by cultural forms, practices, or way of life. Members of a group have a specific affinity with one another because of their similar experience or way of life, which prompts them to associate with one another more than with those not identified with the group, or in a different way. Groups are an expression of social relations; A group exists only in relation to at least one other group. Group identification arises, that is, in the encounter and interaction between social collectivities that experience some differences in their way of life and forms of association, even if they also regard themselves as belonging to the same society" (Young, 1990, p. 43).

[4] *Women's associations and organizations linked to political parties* is the term that I use to navigate the tension between the terms *state feminism* and *institutional feminism*. A wider understanding of the State offers a different interpretation of the term *state feminism*. While the term appears in the existing Greek literature in relation to the autonomous feminists' rhetoric after the socialist party (PASOK) assumed power in 1981, in international feminist scholarly debates (see Mazur & McBride, 2007, 2008; Rai, 2003), the understanding of the state often moves beyond its direct relationship with the government to multiple institutional frameworks. This approach blurs the boundaries between state and institutional feminism and encompasses institutionalized State-oriented practices and discourses beyond a mere correlation with government actions.

chapter IC' refers to punishable actions against the lives of others, and among different categories of homicides the third case refers to abortions and includes three articles. The first law that refers to abortions in the second Greek penal code appeared in 1950 when the political regime was "Crowned Democracy." More specifically, Law 1492/1950 (LHP 11, 1950) for the constitutional validity of the Greek Penal Code situates abortions within crimes against life. In 1978, Karamanlis' right-wing government and Health Minister S. Doxiadis introduced Law 821, allowing abortion until the twelfth week of pregnancy in cases where there was a risk to the mental health of the mother (a psychiatrist would provide the evaluation) and until the twentieth week in case of severe abnormalities of the fetus (Editorial Board, 1979; Avdela et al., 1986, p. 12). Despite the alteration in the related legislations feminists continued their struggle by organizing feminist groups and publishing numerous articles in feminist magazines and magazines of general interest, aiming to provide information about abortion (Avdela et al., 1986, pp. 13–14).

Meanwhile, on March 31, 1979, the International Day of Contraception was celebrated in Greece for the first time. As Avdela, Pappagiannaki, and Sklaveniti (1986) argue, gradually, abortion crossed the limits of the private sphere and was introduced into the Greek public landscape as a social issue. During the second celebration of the International Day of Contraception, ten autonomous women's groups distributed proclamations in public about abortion and contraception. Numerous feminist groups gradually appeared one year later, sharing material with the same concerns (Avdela et al., 1986, p. 15).

In October 1981, the Panhellenic Social Movement (PASOK), the center-left Social-Democratic Party, won the elections and, from the onset, committed itself to "put an end to the unacceptable regime of illegal abortions, with complete and scientific information on family planning, contraception and the decriminalization of abortions" (Avdela et al., 1986, p. 16). The victory of PASOK changed the feminist landscape crucially in Greece, while its commitment to the decriminalization of abortion enabled state feminism to flourish. At the same time, autonomous feminist groups continued to struggle and multiplied in number (Avdela et al., 1986, p. 17).

A turning point in the struggle for legal access to abortion was the Autonomous Women's Movement campaign, which took place in February 1983 and was the first national campaign of the feminist movement in Greece. Their declaration was published alongside the public statement signed by 500 women from all social classes and educational backgrounds who publicly stated that they had had abortions, denouncing the existing regime and demanding immediate decriminalization (PACL 3). The campaign was crucial for two reasons: on the one hand, it was a critical factor in promoting the legalization of abortion, while on the other hand, it led the involved social groups into public conflict.

Indeed, in 1985, seven women who signed the document were interrogated by the police. A demonstration was organized instantly by autonomous feminists who stated, "We are all illegal." There, the Union of Greek Women, with the support of Margarita Papandreou (the wife of the Prime Minister), tried unsuccessfully to cancel the demonstration. At the same time members of religious organizations were also present, claiming that "abortion is a crime." Subsequently, PASOK founded the National Council of Equality. Finally, in May 1986 (LHP 16), a bill was filed in parliament that recognized the right of a pregnant woman to decide freely until the twelfth week whether to carry her pregnancy to term (Avdela et al., 1986, p. 24).

The emergence of the feminist birth control movement, as well as the knowledge that women and feminists produced and circulated, operated as the affective epistemologies of *antimilima*, bringing birth control into the public eye and negotiating its meaning. Inspired by the famous slogan the *personal is politic*al, women transformed abortion and contraception from private and personal issues into public, social, collective, and political concerns. As Athanasiou argues, the Greek feminist birth control movement "was a critique against liberal Democracy and in parallel demand for its radicalizations [...]. The autonomous feminist movement of Metapolitefsi was the demand for a real democratic transition where the gender subjectivities which were not aligned with the ideology of *Fatherland, Religion, Family* would not remain anymore unseen" (2018, p. 23). Here, the demand for a real democratic transition also included the democratization of knowledge, linking women's act of backspeaking with the questioning of epistemic and biopolitical order, medical authority, and institutional forms of knowledge and expertise, not by discrediting them but by finding ways to navigate an unjust world and its problematic conceptual dichotomies.

In that sense, this history cannot be narrowed down only to the history of birth control in Greece or the history of the debate over birth control in the Greek arena. Instead, it is a political history of making knowledge and making *sense* of knowledge; the epistemological history of *antimilima* or the political history of *antimilima* as an *affective epistemology*. It is fabricated through the parallel histories of the politics of knowledge, body politics, and politics of emotions as appeared in the post-dictatorship era in Greece. Thus, *antimilima* is identified as breaking the silence in order for women to un-cover and re-cover. It is the epistemology of survival and breath. It is the critical re-investigation of the boundaries between theory, knowledge, and expertise. This is a history about theory, where affective epistemologies of *antimilima* help us navigate what counts as theory, knowledge, and expertise by challenging and politically reclaiming given and naturalized divisions of theory itself, bodies, concepts, epistemologies, emotions and questioning the hierarchies they produce. But, as Ahmed argues, "theory can do more, the closer it gets to the skin" (2017, p. 10). This process of making *sense* of knowledge describes a world in which the meanings of the concepts are not created by opposing the meanings of other concepts. In other words, affective epistemologies of *antimilima* show how it feels to inhabit a world where the personal is not conceived as the nonpolitical or noncollective, the political is not perceived as the nonpersonal, the scientific is not shaped by the absence of the subjective or the emotional, the emotional is not defined as the unthought, or as distinct from the senses, the theoretical is not constructed in opposition to the body.

The project addresses the following research questions: What counts as knowledge, expertise, and theory? How are hierarchies of knowledge linked to and produced by hierarchies of emotions and subjects? What is the role of the division between reason and emotion, or mind and body, in classifying experience? It reconstructs the history of the Greek feminist birth control movement that emerged in the public landscape directly after the fall of the dictatorial regime (1974) – a social movement active almost everywhere in Greece, from metropolis to suburbs and the countryside, and supported both by women's associations and organizations (linked to political parties) and autonomous feminists.

Affective epistemologies of *antimilima* re-read women's experiential and embodied knowledges that emerged in the blurred boundaries between academia and social movement as acts of backspeaking. They were shaped by fifty-one local feminist groups and women's organizations who developed their expertise in eighteen different physical spaces and expressed their views in eighty-six magazines, publications, and brochures. These groups organized 140 events and maintained ties to 40 international groups and associations. To analyze the complexities of the affective epistemologies of *antimilima,* the Element builds upon theoretical continuities of feminist theory from Donna Haraway to Sara Ahmed, following a theoretical tradition that correlates emotions, senses, experiences, and the body. The Element will explore how all of these contribute to the construction of individual, collective, personal, and political histories.

To navigate this history, we need a map; the theoretical and methodological tools introduced thus far will serve to orient the reader throughout the course of the Element. In Section 1, I discuss the methodological considerations of producing situated knowledges. This section operates as a type of *lens* that is necessary to deeply examine and approach the fragmented history of the affective epistemologies of *antimilima*. The scheme introduced combines approaches from Critical Theory, Sociology, Science Studies, Affect Theory, and Feminist Theory.

Section 2 examines institutional forms of knowledge that were circulated and produced into what I will call an epistemological "regime," a regime then challenged and confronted by affective epistemologies of *antimilima*. To contest an understanding of rational knowledge as unemotional, this section focuses on the affective economies of the Greek birth control debate that were shaped around multiple hegemonic publics – the press, the medical community, politicians, the government, and the Church. I place institutional knowledge in dialogue with emotions, and I discuss hierarchies of emotions, subjects, experiences, and epistemologies to analyze their role in establishing a specific boundary between science and society that excluded women from knowledge production. This discussion is informed by empirical research that analyzes archival material, including magazines and newspapers, textbooks, journals, conference proceedings, laws, regulations, religious and para-ecclesiastical press, and other publications.

Section 3 focuses on the production and circulation of knowledge that shaped women's experiential expertise within the Greek feminist birth control movement. Examining the emotional without confining it to the unthought, the analysis of affective epistemologies of *antimilima* derives from women's and feminists' counterpublics – women's associations and organizations linked to political parties and autonomous feminist groups. Avoiding squeezing experiential expertise into stable categories and typologies (especially with regard to those created to examine/supplement scientific expertise), I follow Sara Ahmed's work and treat the experiential expertise as a sweaty concept to incorporate women's difficulty to challenge the social and epistemological order. This conceptual work – a/the work needed to create a world – reconfigures the relationship between knowledge and experience. The final section puts major takeaways from previous sections into conversation. Bringing women's struggles for reproductive justice into focus, it relocates the feminist critique against the dichotomy between reason and emotion in the interstices between body politics, politics of knowledge, politics of emotions, and biopolitics.

Through the lens of epistemology, *antimilima* therefore opens up different past, current, and future possibilities. In parallel, the combination of different methodological tools alongside an analysis of the rich primary archival collection introduces a conceptual path for examining the relationship between the scientific and the experiential, focused on a type of knowledge that did not reject science but aimed instead at the cooperation among women, society, the state, science, the experts and the Greek health system. This multilevel analysis between history, historiography, and theory reconfigures the rational and the emotional, opening up new possibilities for interpreting and developing democratic knowledge, society, and citizenship.

1 Situated Methodological Considerations

To write about *antimilima* as an affective epistemology is to write about the unstable, the incomplete, and the fragmented. And here, *antimilima* is not an epistemology *despite* being affective but because of it. To write a feminist affective history is to write a history that stains History and a theory that blemishes Theory (see Sedgwick, 1997; Brown, 2001; Stewart, 2008; Athanasiou, 2020; Berlant, 2022). The history of the affective epistemologies of *antimilima* mars these capital-letter disciplines through the (im)possibilities of *not fitting*: as affective in the histories of rationality, as rational in the histories of emotions, as emotional in the histories of the senses and as embodied in the histories of affect. This account of *antimilima* is also constructed by collective experience and the political accountability of *not fitting* into existing social realities shaped by relationships with time and space that are taken for granted: linear temporalities and independent spatialities. The history of the affective epistemologies of *antimilima* reorganizes our relationship with the past, the present, and the future through and within these spatiotemporal interdependencies and our attachments to them. History – as past history, a history of the past, as living history, and as a lived history – needs to connect past experience and present knowledge to explore a collective gendered experience of an era that has not ended (see Chordaki, forthcoming b; Felski, 2002; Halberstam, 2005; Athanasiou & Tzelepis, 2010; Freeman, 2010; Browne, 2014). This history therefore looks at the past with the eyes of the present while directing our gaze toward utopian futures. It situates women's reproductive struggles of the late twentieth century within the political demands and commitments of today's injustice.

In the same way that *antimilima* is situated within broader efforts to reconsider the relationship between the past and the experience of space and time, this history is grounded in a country located in the so-called periphery of Europe, where specific historical and sociopolitical features – localities – exist only within the complex dynamics of the global. It is in precisely this same way that the personal of this history can be realized only through the collective and not as its opposition. Similarly, this is not a history of the gender perspective of birth control but the gendered history of birth control. In this history, gender is not one of the many perspectives of a complex phenomenon but an integral part of it. It is not a history of the production and circulation of knowledge but a history of the knowledge that is produced while it circulates (indicatively see

Hilgartner, 1990; Bensaude-Vincent, 2009; Topham, 2009; Lässig, 2016; Östling et al., 2018; Davies et al., 2019; Halpern, 2019; Lewenstein, 2019).[5]

One needs a fluid, malleable, and unsettled methodology to tell such histories. To write a feminist history *of*, one needs a methodology that reveals the intergenerational character of knowledge and the different embodied and experienced relationships between the past and the present. One needs a methodology that tells a history of the past while producing histories of the present. This dirty methodology of the discomfort and the disloyal (Halberstam, 1998) operates as a type of lens that is necessary to deeply examine and approach theoretically and methodologically the fragmented history of the affective epistemologies of antimilima as they were shaped in the Greek feminist birth control movement. The introduced scheme combines approaches from Affect Theory, Critical Theory, Sociology, Science Studies, and Feminist/Queer Theory.

This methodology is fragile enough to create a narration that shatters the mechanisms of mediation between knowledge and experience/emotions. To do that, it incorporates what Papanikolaou calls "the archive trouble" (2018), Lee defines as the "queer/ed archival methodology" (2017), Eichhorn suggests as the "archival turn in feminism" (2013), Marshall and Tortorici describe as the process of "turning archival" (2022) and Foster explains as the "archival impulse" (2004). *Archive trouble* allows bodies, emotions, and senses to shape primary archival collections around women's struggles against epistemic and reproductive injustice. It is through the re-reading of personal trauma and pain as collective experience that new attachments shape archives that direct us toward the reconstruction of gendered social relationships. These archives can make visible the unseen, hear the silenced, memorialize the forgotten, touch the untouchable, and navigate the abstract. Such continuously-in-progress archives move between different affects while they produce knowledge through and with the bodies. They are the surfaces upon which histories are disrupted and orders are disordered – where the "biopolitical noise" emerges (Papanikolaou, 2018, p. 172). This is the *queer/ed archival* body – the body of knowledge that produces knowledge for the bodies that unhinge epistemic and affective hierarchies (see Lee, 2017, p. 9). Such archives materialize resistance on the surfaces of the (in)complete. Eichhorn argues that they describe the process of "putting the outrage in order" (p. 157) by resituating past experiences to contemporary struggles (p. 4). They reconstruct inter- and intra-generational bonds while shaping genealogical politics through the links they produce

---

[5] For a brief history of abortion discourses, see Vassili 2022; for a sociological analysis see Chalkia 2007; for a critical anthropological account on birth control and demographic imaginaries, see Athanasiou 2001.

between different forms of (historical) knowledge. Feminist archives allow us to shape our genealogies beyond the given cultural and epistemic divisions that have alienated our positionalities. Such archives move through bodies and allow bodies to move through them, turning objects into knowledges and permitting feelings and emotions to redirect our bodies and make new worlds (Marshall & Tortorici, 2022, pp. 8,12).

The feminist birth control movement is its archives, which continuously produce politics of resistance. This movement as a history did not stop or end in the past, but it is reconstructed again and again when sexual and reproductive oppression occurs. It continues to exist every moment we (re)turn to it while we aim to rebuild archives of reproductive justice. The archives of the Greek feminist birth control movement describe the noise, discomfort, and unsettledness that took place in post-dictatorial Greek society, allowing us to revisit Metapolitefsi through a feminist "desire for history" (Hesford, 2013, p. 7). They also allow us to navigate the multiple temporalities in which feminist explorations reach the displaced – the affective places that disposition vulnerable histories (see Foster, 2004).

Affective epistemologies of *antimilima* allow us to find the displaced history of knowledge within the rigid history of human rights. Similarly, they allow us to find the displaced archives of birth control within the archives of the multiple histories around them. For this history, the archives include the Delfis Archival Center, the Library on Gender and Equality, E. Leontidou's private archival collection, the Library of the Hellenic Society of Gynecology and Obstetrics, the Library of the Medical School of Athens, the Association of Midwives of Athens, The Library of the Hellenic Parliament, the Contemporary Social Archives, the Hellenic Statistical Authority, Eurostat, the National Center of Sociale Research and the National Documentation Center. More specifically, these archives include magazines and newspapers of general interest, medical textbooks, journals and conference proceedings, laws, regulations, transcripts of conversations that took place in parliament, conservative and religious press, women's and feminists' publications and translations, exchanges with other feminist birth control movements around the globe, pamphlets, proclamations, posters, flyers, and publications by women's associations and organizations linked to political parties and autonomous feminist groups.

Antimilima takes place. Affective epistemologies of *antimilima* have their own spatialities. These are the places and spaces where knowledge is produced and circulated within and through its affective attachments. To make affective epistemologies of *antimilima* visible, one needs a methodology that deconstructs spatial divisions, questions hegemonic analytical categories, and, thus, disrupts the hierarchies of emotions linked to epistemological classifications.

Here, Fraser's (1995) and Warner's (2005) publics and counterpublics show the distribution of knowledge (through its complex relation with emotion and experience) in different social and epistemic realms. Put differently, if we conceive the practices of production and circulation of knowledge as separate and chronologically different processes, epistemic and social hierarchies are produced. To fight this hegemonic theoretical scheme, one must prioritize epistemic visibility, which will result in the visibility of marginal and oppressed social groups and blur the boundaries of academia and social movements. Crucially, the notion of the public must be constructed beyond that of the nonprivate and within its multiplicity.

Feminist critiques have analyzed the complex character of the public sphere in correlation to the gendered relationship between the public and the private. This discourse draws on Constructionist Theory and links the notion of the public sphere to numerous analytical categories such as equality, accessibility, reconfiguration of natural categories, and a multiplicity of standpoints. Ferre et al. (2002, p. 307) argue that questioning dominant categories can reveal hidden inequalities and achieve social equality. The pluralist model, discussed by Benson (2009, p. 178), emphasizes diversity and inclusion in public discourse, highlighting the importance of peripheral voices. Such critical approaches to the public sphere emerged in the second half of the twentieth century as a response to Habermasian theory, which emphasized the gendered meanings that construct the concept of the public sphere itself (Geoff, 2002).

Feminism has questioned the dichotomy between private and public, exposing its naturalization and exclusionary nature, thus allowing for women's visibility and multiple experiences to exist within the public sphere. The Habermasian public sphere has been criticized for idealization, exclusion, and ignoring other forms of counterpublicity or competing public spheres (indicatively see Negt & Kluge 1988). Fraser links it to the presence of a bourgeois, masculinist, white supremacist public sphere and emphasizes the ignorance of the internal organization and structures of public deliberation (1995). The common understanding of the public sphere designates a gendered domain that historically has not guaranteed equal participation for every social group (see Hawkesworth, 2006; Susen, 2011). The problematic character of Habermas' notion of the public sphere has also been associated with tensions between the right to speak and the right to be heard (Pajnik, 2006). The feminist symmetry between these two recognizes the parallel demands for discourse, action, and responsibility. This symmetry is a way to stress the importance of gender in communication and question which forms and actors become visible or dominant in the gendered public sphere.

To unsettle publicity as the surface where embodied attachments of epistemological and emotional bodies take place is to approach publics "[as] queer creatures [that] you cannot point to them, count them or look at them in the eye. You cannot avoid them; they have become an almost natural feature of the social landscape, like pavement. [. . .] Much of the texture of the modern social life lies in the invisible presence of the publics that flit around us like large, corporate ghosts" (Warner, 2005, p. 7). The emotional and thus political work of putting an "s" to the notion of the public (see Chordaki forthcoming a) examines the differences among coexisting spheres and the dichotomy between publics and (Fraser's, 1995) counterpublics/subaltern counterpublics or (Susen, 2011) counterhegemonic realms. This work describes the agony of finding what is left after the deconstruction of the public as it has been constructed through the private. As Butler argues, it is the shape of the closet that produces the expectation of the outside and, at the same time, ensures the inability to fulfill this expectation (1993, p. 309) – and this is the feminist exploration beyond it.

This political shift in the conceptualization of the notion of the public sphere is crucial. It allows us to *see* numerous central and peripheral actors – and the gender power relations among them – their involvement in the production and circulation of knowledge, their role in the creation of meanings in regard to what was considered public or private in a given historical period, and the impact of these categories on the (in)visibility of certain types of knowledge. It allows us to describe the process of making *sense* of knowledge because it reorganizes experience. This shift reveals the publics and counterpublics of birth control in Greece. The publics include the press (magazines and newspapers of general interest), the debate among social groups that were involved (women and feminists, the medical community, politicians, journalists, anti-choice supporters, and others), the medical community, politicians, and government and religious groups (anti-choice supporters). The counterpublics are composed of the women's associations and organizations linked to political parties and autonomous feminist groups.

Making *sense* of knowledge is critically revisiting the (dis)orders and the interdependencies between experiences, emotions, senses, knowledges, and subjects. In this sense, affective epistemologies of *antimilima* are the movements through the attachments that arise within such interdependencies. These movements continuously create spaces, smaller or bigger. As flows, they move to fit and freeze to block. Such traces are space-making, meaning-making, and ways of knowing. They are also ways of communicating. Communication in affective epistemologies of *antimilima* is identified to both the production and circulation of knowledge. It is shaped through the movement and the absence of movement, the presence and the absence, the verbal and the nonverbal, the flow and the blockage of flow. But what has it left when the "absent is not identified as the not being present?" (Jones et al., 2015) What type of experiences and relationships arise through the nonbinary conception of silence? To fully explore affective epistemologies of *antimilima,* one needs to theorize the tensions of the concept of silence – that are the ways through which the flow and the blockage of flow reorganize the space, mobilize emotions and "reinforce power relations by demarcating territories where acts, people, and ideas can (not) belong" (Jones et al., p. 1) – that is the "absence of presence and the presence of absence" (Cresswell, 1996).

Affective epistemologies of *antimilima* describe intergenerational bodies of knowledges about birth control – those that resist as being "distant, silent, unspoken, obscured" (Jones et al., 2015, p. 2. See also, Athanasiou, 2017; Avramopoulou, 2017). This type of resistance that comes from silence can create noise, which, as Kallio argues, can be transformed into voice (2015, p. 3). Nevertheless, these epistemologies are also the answer to the silent voices that become noises. These parallel phenomena and the tensions between silences and noises that took place within and around the feminist birth control movement are "political silences that loudly vie for responses" (Dingli & Cooke, 2019, p. 1) and political voices that silently ignore the questions. As Davies and Irvine argue, silence can describe one's "difficulty to talk or the lack of language" (2022, p. 6), but it can also describe the power of domination and the ability to exclude. Here, silence is perceived both as practice and action and as a signal (Vieira, 2020), but far and for most, it is political – it is a mode of political communication (Vieira et al., 2019), a form of political being (Vieira, 2020a) and "much more than the space between words – it is a political category in its own right. As we do things with words, so silence too allows us to act politically. Silence can acquiesce to power as well as deploy it. It can claim authority as well as constitute community. There is meaning in what is said but also in what was left unsaid, in the silences speech harbors, in the refusal to speak. What powers and potentials lie in silence?"[6]

Multiple moments of silence (of other social groups) as political performative acts placed within the context of patriarchy that blocked the circulation of knowledge and reproduced gender discrimination in multiple ways. Moreover, due to the division in medical terminology regarding abortions in the Greek language (see discussion on ektrosi/amvlosi), the politics of silence offer an explanation for the multiple ways in which scientific and medical culture have been shaped historically. Last, to perceive silence beyond the binary economies of presence and absence can reveal how women's silent positions empowered them and transformed their personal experiences (of trauma) surrounding abortion and contraception into hope directed toward the

---

[6] For more see: http://monicabritovieira.com/thepoliticsofsilence/

collective political demand for the feminization-as-demasculinization of OB/GYN that included women's engagement with science.

Affective epistemologies of *antimilima* occur within the Greek feminist birth control movement, and to locate the former, we need to approach the latter as a *boundary movement* that operates both inside and outside the boundaries of science – in terms of knowledge, culture, practice, and institutions. *Boundary movements*, functioning as an analytical framework, shed light on the blurring of lines between professionals and lay activists, facilitating a shift in roles, and thereby politicizing physicians and professionalizing lay activists (Joffe et al., 2004, p. 776). This framework views social movements as dynamic and multifaceted, traversing cultural and analytical spheres that extend across varied social contexts and bodies of knowledge (McCormick et al., 2003, p. 547). More precisely, *boundary movements* focus on dismantling the boundaries between scientific and nonscientific realms of knowledge and between expert professionals and laypersons. Furthermore, they contribute to the understanding of social movements by highlighting the intricate relationship between science and civil society (McCormick et al., 2003, p. 547, See also, Brown et al., 2004, p. 65). Several case studies connect *boundary movements* with grassroots women's health movements, where individual experiences are emphasized and become a pivotal tool in both political and scientific contexts (McCormic et al., 2003).

Consequently, personal experiences are translated into public issues. There is a phased involvement of so-called laypeople in science: first, by gaining access to scientific knowledge and second, by bridging their own knowledge with scientific findings (McCormick et al., 2003, p. 571). Analyses of the significance of Health Social Movements (HSMs) within the histories of science and gender studies underscore the relationship between women's experiences and science on a public scale while emphasizing the communal nature of scientific knowledge. Since the 1960s, critiques from feminist HSMs have brought attention to various issues pertinent to the history of science. These include the unchallenged acceptance of medical knowledge, decision-making processes whereby technoscience dictates social policy, and the credibility and power of scientific knowledge. *Boundary movements* bring the politically and epistemologically important dichotomies of identities and knowledges into the center of attention, allowing us to reposition ourselves in the (given) distance between emotions and reason.

Affective epistemologies of *antimilima* are emotional, sensorial, and rational. Sara Ahmed's theory of emotions allows us to approach them as such. As Athanasiou (2020) and Avramopoulou (2018) argue, in Ahmed's work, emotions hold an epistemological status in which affect can be critically resituated within the complex mesh of the social, the political, and thus the theoretical. In this way, emotions are both social and embodied, without producing any kind of epistemic hierarchies between them, and are both a way of knowing and a way of world-making. Indeed, in her work, Ahmed creates a unique scheme for theorizing feminist experiences – she creatively explains the relationships and relationalities between the body, the world, and theory when she argues that we produce knowledge through the experiences we acquire from existing in the world *as* feminists (2018). Such experiences are affective *as* sensorial and rational.

For Ahmed, the political importance of theorizing emotions is based on the question of what emotions *do* rather than what they *are* (2004, p. 4). As she argues, emotions circulate between bodies, stick/attach while they move, and take shape from the contact we have with objects; they are oriented or disoriented toward/away (from) something; They are related to the sensation of feelings and their interpretations. They can be pedagogical and open up lines of communication; they are bound up with stories of justice and injustice; they are effects and not origins; they are distributed in time and space, and they make communities (see Ahmed, 2004, 2010, 2017, 2018a).

Body, world, and theory unsettle what epistemologies might look alike. To wander is to unsettle. For Ahmed, the act of wandering is precisely what we need to imagine a world away from given binaries. She writes, "The body opens up as the world opens up before it – the body unfolds into the unfolding of a world that becomes approached as another body" (2004, p. 180). In this scheme, emotions, epistemologies, and experiences are more than bound to political commitments. The primary political commitment of affective epistemologies of *antimilima* is to reorient the status of knowledge to the emotional beyond the unthought, the rational beyond the unemotional, the experiential beyond the nonscientific, and the sensorial beyond the nonaffective. Emotions, as Ahmed argues, are critical epistemologies themselves and are linked to the organization of different forms of knowledges. This means that they mobilize movements between the different forms of knowledges – in terms of domination or marginalization – while they (emotions) are shaped as they circulate and stick to bodies of knowledge.

Ahmed argues that emotions are attributed to communities as the former are distributed unequally in spaces. As emotions are perceived as the Other of Reason, they become subordinated, classified, and stick to bodies while they produce hierarchies among themselves (2004, pp. 2–4). Emotions are related to power relations and the domination of certain truths over others. What she calls *pathologized emotionality of femininity* has been constructed in relation to the *problematic rationality of masculinity*. And it is precisely this correlation that produces the translation of hierarchies of emotions to the hierarchies of knowledges and subjects (and vice versa) (2004, p. 170). Ahmed argues that emotions cannot be separated from the bodily world of feeling and sensation. They are bound up with all those feelings that are felt on the bodily surface – the skin surface where we touch and are touched by the world. And the "truths of this world are depended on emotions, on how they move subjects and stick them together" (Ahmed, 2004, pp. 170–71). Affective epistemologies of *antimilima* shape how we make *sense* of the world around us as it is shaped through the process of making *sense*.

Along these lines, Ahmed's theoritization of emotions provides the necessary framework to approach affective epistemologies of *antimilima* – through the notion of *sweaty concept* – as the *experiential expertise* that women developed within the feminist birth control movement. Nevertheless, it also allows us to conceive them as acts of resistance that confronted the *affective economies of birth control*.

Sweaty concepts (Ahmed, 2014) are what allow us to reconstruct the concept of experiential expertise in a way that will include affective epistemologies of *antimilima,* which will be aligned to other forms of knowledge. As I have shown elsewhere (Chordaki, 2022, 2024), experiential expertise has become a central focus within the theoretical discourse of many disciplines, such as Science Studies, Health Studies, Feminist and Disability Science Studies, Design and Arts, Peace and Conflict Studies, and Geography. Through a careful analysis of the language, research questions, and the methodological demands of each discipline, I have concluded that while the concept has several meanings and connotations according to its disciplinary boundaries, shared among them is the recognition of methodological and analytical challenges encountered by academics in their attempts to discuss, identify, and evaluate experiential expertise (Chordaki, 2022, 2024).[7]

The process of categorizing and classifying experiential knowledge and expertise often involves employing various methodological tools. These tools, while beneficial, may have inherent limitations that make them unsuitable for comprehensive analysis of experiential expertise, which is characterized by its complexities, malleability, intersubjectivity, and other qualities that defy measurement and neat classification. Through *sweaty concepts*, distinctions between

---

[7] Experiential expertise takes on a number of different definitions according to different disciplines: as the other of the scientific (see Flinterman et al., 2001; Collins & Evans, 2002; 2007; Kennedy 2015; Wynne & Lynch, 2015; Blume 2016) as a concept that is oriented in Health Care Systems and Service (see Inhorne & Whittle, 2001; D'Agincourt-Canning, 2005; Castro et al., 2019), the embodied knowledge in action, the idiosyncratic or relational way of knowing (indicatively see Borkman, 1976; Fisher, 2007; Durbin, 2011; Nijs & Heylinghen, 2015; Rice et al., 2015; Azocar & Ferree, 2016; Julian et al., 2019; Nimkulrat et al., 2020).

practice and theory, as well as between knowledge and expertise, can be avoided, fostering a more symmetrical relationship between the researcher, historical subjects, and the object of study, allowing the concept of experiential expertise to be shaped beyond the ideology of heterodeterminism. Conversely, efforts to rigidly fit experiential expertise into analytical frameworks designed for scientific expertise risk marginalizing the nuanced qualities of the former that cannot be adequately addressed using tools designed for the latter.

Ahmed's *sweaty concepts* offer new ways of understanding embodied experiences that do not conform to conventional language or social norms. They provide a way to explore the challenges of navigating spaces where our knowledge is not acknowledged and our experience is not considered valid. Through this approach, Ahmed encourages us to embrace our knowledge's fluidity and vulnerability and consider how our experiences shape our understanding of the world. Put differently, this approach provides a path for "giving words to re-describe a situation" (Ahmed, 2014) by juxtaposing dominant histories and healing our traumatic experiences of exclusion caused by language (Athanasiou, 2020). Treating experiential expertise as a *sweaty concept* embodies methodologically the difficulty of talking about, locating, and analyzing experiential expertise, and it disentangles the concept from an "other" of scientific expertise. As such, it allows for the exploration of women's knowledge and expertise derived from a marginalized social position, from an invisible space, and from a *protesting* body that suffers and is not situated in a familiar place – (what Ahmed calls) home. As she states, sweaty concepts are a way to understand how feminist knowledge is produced from bodies and returns to them in order to transform their experiences of phenomena (Ahmed, 2014, pp. 49–51).

While *sweaty concepts* help to understand women's and feminist experiential expertise beyond the reason/emotion binary, Ahmed's concept of *affective economies* is the analytical framework from which I will draw for the analysis of the complex and multilayered processes of the construction of the birth control debate in Greece. *Affective economies* will demonstrate how embedded, gendered power relationships polarized the birth control debate, resulting in the construction of hierarchies of emotions, subjects, and knowledge, as well as the de-struction of the epistemologies of *antimilima*. "How do emotions work to align some subjects with some others and against other others? How do emotions move between bodies?" Ahmed asks (2018). In order to explain how emotions shape bodies while they circulate between them, she coins the term "affective economies" and argues for the affective process that aligns individuals to communities, social spaces, and embodied spaces (p. 132). For Ahmed, affective economies show how emotions are not a property of the body, but rather are produced *because* they circulate. In this sense, emotions reorganize the positionality of figures in space as they circulate between them and stick them together.

Intentional (directed) and relational emotions attached to bodies (i.e., the nation) or bodies of knowledge (i.e., science) create surfaces and boundaries between science and society and/or the private and public, and the multiple publics. As constructed boundaries, such demarcations are subjected to power relations and constant negotiations while creating a specific relationship between different institutional forms of knowledge and experience: established forms of knowledge classify experience, and this classification of experience and affect reassure specific forms of knowledge. This co-production of knowledge and the processes of classification of experience took place within the affective economies of the birth control debate, where emotions shaped networks, performativity, and power by defining the alleged boundary between science and society, women's relationship to knowledge and expertise, and the hegemonic meaning of birth control.

This methodology ensures that affective epistemologies of *antimilima* will flourish freely. It confirms that our theoretical scheme allows them to escape. Let me allow them to *escape*.

2 *Againstness*: Affective Economies and the Birth Control Debate

Affective epistemologies of *antimilima*, as a collective act of resistance, require the analysis of *something* that women and feminists confronted during the Metapolitefsi period. That *something* is the distribution of established forms of knowledge across a variety of public spheres. Such publics included the press, the medical community, the political sphere, and the Church. These were the primary interlocutors for debates surrounding birth control in Greece. After the fall of the dictatorial regime, the first feminist efforts to bring attention to women's experiences with birth control emerged, sparking a public debate. Various actors from diverse social backgrounds, including journalists, doctors, politicians, and clerics, shaped this debate by circulating institutional knowledge about birth control within their respective spheres of influence.

Through Ahmed's concept of affective economies, I will demonstrate the role of emotions in the production and circulation of knowledge and the conceptualization of birth control. I discuss hierarchies of emotions, subjects, experiences, and epistemologies to analyze their role in establishing a specific boundary between science and society that excluded women from knowledge production. I doing so, I use Ahmed's theoretical/methodological concept of *alignment*.

This empirical research analyzes archival material, including magazines and newspapers, textbooks, journals, conference proceedings, laws, regulations, religious and para ecclesiastical Press, and publications.

For this research, I examined 715 references related to birth control between 1974 and 1991 in magazines and newspapers of general interest, focusing on who – as well as what, when, and how – circulated and produced knowledge about birth control through the circulation of emotions.[8] I also focused on the circulation of emotions within abortion regulations. Furthermore, I examined medical textbooks, conference proceedings, and scientific journals that trained doctors and addressed the medical community, examining how emotions stick to scientific knowledge. The study also includes 100 articles published between 1978 and 1987 in religious/para ecclesiastical Press concerning birth control in order to get a sense of the circulation of emotions and knowledge in anti-choice groups.

I am interested in thinking with Ahmed about how emotions worked in the Greek Metapolitefsi to *align* specific social groups against others, specific conceptualizations to dominate others, and specific bodies of knowledge to work against others. I am also interested in exploring how all these were differentiated within and between multiple publics, what kind of discourses and practices mobilized, and which relationships mediated these discourses. One goal of this study is to examine how such *alignments* shaped the boundaries between different social realms, social groups and subjects, and epistemologies.

The Greek public debate surrounding birth control, spanning from 1974 to 1991, was enacted primarily through articles authored by journalists. These articles analyzed various topics such as abortion, contraception, sterilization, family planning, legislation, and male perspectives. The peak of the discussion, occurring from 1984 to 1987, concentrated on abortion and contraception, with a particular emphasis on presenting pro-choice and anti-choice viewpoints alongside discussions on law, international news, and abortion rates in Greece. Pro-choice articles mainly presented the State as the regulator and protector of reproductive rights, and they claimed *for* women the vulnerable position of a subject in need of protection by law. In these narratives, concern and fear for women's health were pitted against the feelings of guilt, hypocrisy,

---

[8] There is an unequal distribution of the published articles in the magazines and newspapers of general interest. While they start appearing in 1974 (in parallel with the first feminist struggles), most of them are published between 1984 and 1987, a phenomenon that can be explained by the campaign of the Autonomous Women's Movement that started in 1983 and was accompanied by the public statement of 500 women who declared that they had aborted illegally, phenomena that resulted in the climax of the public debate.

humiliation, and shame generated by the illegal birth control regime (indicatively see Mesimvrini 1, 1983). In many cases, journalists admired women's courage and power to renegotiate the boundary between pain and pleasure in their sexual experiences through discourses about birth control. Such a reorientation was understood as a response to the violence, injustice, and oppression women often experienced. Here, agony and fear against the continuous and repeated illegal regime of abortion (ektrosadika) aligned the demand for the decriminalization of abortion to a body of demands that included family planning, sex education and the protection of motherhood. But for most decriminalization appeared as synonymous to women's right to reinvent their bodies (altering men's attitudes toward them) and establish more equal relationships with men (indicatively see Kefala, 1984; Rixi 1, 1984). Fear and concern also aligned abortion and the need to protect unwanted pregnancy with the feeling of responsibility toward other members of society, including both men and women. Such narratives stood against those that promoted the decriminalization of abortion but silenced its correlation to women's struggles for bodily autonomy. These opposing narratives approached decriminalization only through ideas of progress, civilization, wellbeing, concepts that were related European visions that Greece aspired to appropriate (indicatively, Pantheon 2, 1986).

In several cases, anger about power and gendered power relations mobilized critical alignments. Abortions aligned with women's liberation, while at the same time, women's struggles for self-determination operated against the alignment of birth control with plunging birth rates that threatened an ethnonationalist idea of the Greek state. In this way, the movement for decriminalization and bodily autonomy worked to detach women's bodies from narratives of reproductive anxiety that had transformed birth into a national issue and treated women as reproductive machines whose duty was to eliminate external threats against the nation (indicatively, see Farakos, 1985; To Vima 6, 1985).

In many articles, journalists presented the encounters between different groups of pro-choice and anti-choice supporters, allowing for the circulation of diverse emotions and the conflicted meanings of birth control that emerged. Within public debate, women's fear and uncertainty over their reproductive freedom were often attached to psychosomatic responses, especially in cases where they had to face hateful rhetoric and threats of anti-choice supporters, including the assertion that abortion is murder. In such narratives of anti-choice supporters, the circulation of positive emotions, such as love, was often directed to children and attached to the sense of care toward (unprotected) mothers. However, this love was also transformed into hate and violence that oriented anti-choice supporters toward ideas for the creation of detention centers for women struggling with unwanted pregnancies and (unwanted) children. Here, the fear of pro-choice supporters' for their autonomy aligned them against the anti-choice supporters, who often identified the former with the vulnerable position of other social groups such as African Americans, Arabs, immigrants, soldiers, and students. Within the narratives of anti-choice supporters, the love toward children, the institution of family, the Greek population, and the nation itself were unified by their enmity toward these other bodies. Through their abortions or demands for the decriminalization of abortions, women threaten the aforementioned anti-choice ideas (Damianidi, 1986). According to anti-choice rhetoric abortions are catalyzed the fear of population decline, the external threat of national enemies such as the Turks, and the internal threat of women who had aborted. At the same time, Greek society, Orthodoxy, and anti-choice are conceived in the same narratives as interchangeable.

Discussions about contraception in articles focused on the pill and other contraceptive methods are mostly appeared between1985 and 1988. Feelings of hesitation, trust, and distrust aligned this specific contraceptive method with the presentation of side effects and contraindications that range from cancer to blood clots, cardiac diseases, blood pressure issues, and mental health issues. This correlation produced a particular conceptualization that dominated public debate and presented the pill as a "curse or a miracle" (Bioubi, 1976) or "double-edged sword in relation to abortion" (Pantheon 1, 1981). On the other hand, feelings of trust in science conceptualized the pill as a revolutionary method that brought together, according to the authors, diverse demands: Western women's need for autonomy and third-world low-income families' need to control the size of their families, ignoring often that the latter was a western demand (To Vima 2, 1985).

In articles related to the presentation of different contraceptive methods and experimental ones, emotions appear to be crucial both for the classification of different contraceptive methods and for the conceptualization of contraception itself. Classification of the different contraceptive methods included different criteria that resulted in listing the methods, usually but not always in relation to their effectiveness or harmfulness. The combination between classification, criteria, and conceptualization of contraception was accompanied by the circulation of multiple emotions. Stress and anxiety that women experience while using the withdrawal/pull-out method make the latter to be ranked very low in comparison with other methods. In parallel, concern for women's health often lines up the suitability of the methods to their ethical classification, including the expected women's relationships to motherhood and marriage. Interestingly, in some cases contraceptive methods are judged according to the possibility that they leave open for women to have multiple partners – a risky sexual behavior that was associated with the increase of the risk of contracting an STD. Narratives related to the emergency pill accompany the presentation of contraceptive methods with the hesitation that often women and Greek society have against contraception based on the fear they feel that the latter will liberate the former from the stress of pregnancy, disordering the given sexual social orders. In contrast, trust in science conceptualizes contraception by utilizing different criteria about their categorization that differ from efficacy rates, the possible subject that holds the responsibility for each method, and doctors' critical role in choosing the appropriate contraceptive method for each woman (indicatively, see Gynaika, 1982; To Vima 1, 1984; Eleftherotypia 2, 1984).

Male contraception aligns with the continuous need to secure men's feelings of happiness and pleasure as the ultimate criterion that shapes scientific research. Further scientific research is driven perpetually by the disappointment of the medical community in its current inability to comprehensively fulfill this expectation. Such feelings of disappointment were attached to the perception of the male bodies as complex (to understand and intervene) mechanisms that are compared and contradicted to the accessible female bodies through which female fertility could be easily controlled (see Bioubi, 1976; Eleftherotypia 1, 1983).

Articles in the press also reflected women's and feminists' involvement in the birth control debate and appeared mainly between 1983 and 1986. These pieces presented arguments and opinions from women's organizations, autonomous feminist groups, individual women, and coalitions regarding birth control. They also discussed conflicts, political participation, recordings of women's experiences, and the organization of related events. However, the predominant focus was on the prosecution of seven feminists following public statements by women who had abortions, as well as Margaret Papandreou's involvement and subsequent reactions from opposing organizations and groups. Despite the relative prominence of certain women's organizations, autonomous feminist groups also received coverage in magazines and newspapers.

Women's organizations (see Federation of Greek Women, Greek League for Women's Rights, Union of Greek Women, Democratic Women's Movement, etc.) focused more on the importance of feeling safe, an emotion that was attached to concern over women's health. This correlation between safety and concern was responsible for aligning abortion with decriminalization efforts, both of which would be accompanied by the development of state-controlled family planning programs and the circulation of contraception. For them safety also meant the engagement of the medical community and experts in related advisory stations and clinics (Valasi, 1985; Kyriakatiki Eleftherotypia 7, 1981; Eleftheros Typos 1, 1983. See also, Pantheon 3, 1984). On the contrary, autonomous groups (see the Autonomous Women's Movement, the Club of

Piraeus, the House of Women in Athens, the Group of Women's Bookstore, the Groups of Imitos and Ampelokipoi, etc.) circulated their anger and indignation toward discourses and practices that were taken their own right to control their bodies. This phenomenon aligned abortions to contraception and sexuality and, consequently, transforming birth control as a tool that empowers women and protect them from the idea that their anatomy is also their destiny. Women who stood for the decriminalization of abortions allowed the emotional complexity of their experiences to create a counter-alignment against the performative connection between illegal abortion and women's silent, passive position toward medical authorities. Additionally, there were narratives linked to people's love toward the Greek nation, connecting births and nationalism, in which contraception aligned with financial and demographic data related to population decline/anxieties and state-controlled family planning. Against such discourses, women counter-aligned contraception with the control of their reproductivity, self-determination, and free expression of sexuality (indicatively, see Papastathopoulou, 1983a; Rixi 2, 1983; Ta Nea 1, 1983; Eleftherotypia 3, 1984).

Women's participation in the press debate focused on amplifying the courage of those who publicly shared their abortion experiences, prompting societal and governmental responses. Additionally, it addressed the fear surrounding unsafe, illegal abortions, leading to the formation of feminist coalitions on national, international, and transnational levels. Coalitions such as those between the Autonomous Women's Movement and the International Planned Parenthood Federation, the Women's Global Network on Reproductive Rights (PACL 4, 1986) or the Women's International Information and Communication Service (DEC 3, 1981) struggled to secure women's reproductive rights and transform individual struggles into collective, safe experiences (Kazakopoulou, Papastathopoulou, 1984; Mpenou, 1985).

Articles in the press reflecting doctors' perspectives primarily focused on abortion, contraception, sterilization, and family planning, mainly between 1984 and 1986. Notably, discussions about abortion and contraception dominate these articles. Doctors expressed views both for and against the decriminalization of abortion, all driven by concern for women's health and love of life. In cases of pro-choice supporters, love of life was directed at women's lives, while the need to lower the abortion rate prioritized issues of population decline in Greece and visions of modernization. For the anti-choice supporters, the love of life referred to the supposed fetus' life, while the demand to lower abortion rates continued to be linked with the population decline in Greece.

Characteristically, a doctor supported the decriminalization of abortions because "they offer calmness to lost women's consciousness, something that doctors experience as well" (Apolopoulou, 1986). Another doctor argued that abortion is not a criminal act when doctors perform it, but that it remains an unethical act to terminate the fetus' life (To Vima 4, 1986). Such examples show how compassion as a collective emotion felt by the medical community constructs women who have aborted as "lost." By contrast, the medical community and the State act as saviors. The very same emotions of empathy indeed directed in many cases the medical community toward the support for the decriminalization of abortion. However, this linkage between empathy and the right for women to get safe abortions, operated at the same time as the surface in which the moral character of the act emerges and is linked to the authority of the experts. Experts appear as those who are responsible for practicing safe abortions and have the moral accountability of an unethical act. Similarly, while presenting the methods of abortion (curettage) alongside risks and possible complications, feelings of care toward the female body detach it from women as subjects, aligning abortions to miscarriages in cases of early sexual relations and multiple partners. As a doctor states, "All the above do not help the uterus to calm" (To Vima 5, 1985).

Furthermore, doctors' opinions regarding contraception were mainly focused on the pill, its advantages and disadvantages. Here, hesitation and fear toward the technology of the pill orient doctors against women for not trusting contraception. At the same time, the same feelings circulate hesitation and fear among the medical community and become attached to feelings of concern regarding women's ability to become mothers when the pill interferes with reproduction. When this shift takes place, contraception and the pill are also aligned with the exhortation: "Women quit the pill!" (indicatively, see Ethnos 1, 1987). Interestingly, in those references (articles reflecting doctors' views), only three articles describe different contraceptive methods, which indicates that concern over women's health and sexual pleasure was not able to align contraception to the circulation of the related knowledge but instead circulated merely a plethora of opinions about the pill (Mahairopoulou, 1982; Mpredakis, 1986). Additionally, in the presentation of two sterilization methods, vasectomy and laparoscopy, discussion of the former describes men's feelings toward the procedure, while the discussion of the latter focuses on the efficacy of the procedure (Mpredakis, 1986). Finally, in relation to the concept of family planning, the promotion of contraception, sterilization, and sex education is aligned with the creation of "responsible partners and happy families." It is precisely this alignment that detaches contraception from reproductive control and transforms it into an antidote for abortion: "Contraception will decrease abortion rates [...], but we have never told a woman 'come to get contraception in order not to have children' – instead we urge women not to have abortions" (Eleftherotypia 4, 1985).

Within the articles on birth control published in the press, there were also those written from/referring to the politicians who mainly presented their opinions or reported on parliament proceedings that resulted in the creation of new (abortion) laws. Such articles were primarily published between 1985 and 1986 and were mobilized by a collective assertion that the State should secure not only women's safety but also the feeling of safety for women. This feeling was negotiated within the contradictory argumentations about the decriminalization of abortion. On the one hand, legal abortion was aligned to women's health, the prevention of unsafe abortions, gender equality, the promotion of childcare, and family care. On the other, it was attached to the love of the fetus, aligning it with family support, social services for multi-child parents and the development of family planning services within the "Christian spirit" (indicatively, see Avgi, 1986; Avriani, 1986; Eleftheros Typos 2, 1986). Similarly, the demand to alter the law aligned ministries, medical unions/associations, and women's organizations. Anti-choice supporters circulated their anxiety about population decline – what Athanasiou calls the "demographic anxieties over the nation's future" (2006), transforming the State into a savior for the nation's problems instead of women's problems. Such anti-choice arguments, as developed by some politicians, were presented as the "real problems of our society" (that were correlated to corruption, drugs, threats against the institution of the family, and radioactivity) and contradicted the fake problems of abortions, aligning humanism and democracy with the fetus' life and rights (Mesimvrini 2, 1986; Apogevmatini 1, 1986; Apogevmatini Kyriakis, 1986).

Other articles in the press presented the opinions of anti-choice supporters, priests, and organizations. Such articles mainly appeared in 1986 and discussed either priests' opinions toward the decriminalization of abortion or the organization of public events and demonstrations held by the Church and religious groups against the new bill that decriminalized abortions. Such arguments were derived mainly from love of family, life, and the need to protect single mothers, and they likened abortion to crime, since life was believed to begin at conception (indicatively, see Thourios, 1981; Ta Nea 3, 1984; Metropolitan Timotheos, 1985). In such narratives, abortion law was perceived as responsible for aligning the State against the Church and the Holy Synod, the scientific community, Greek society, the law of God, and the ethics of the bible. In such cases it (the law) was characterized as ethnocidal, similar to bloodletting and slaughter and identified as the funeral of Greece (Apogevmatini 2, 1986; Vradini 2, 1986). This tragedy, as appeared in many priests' arguments, aligned the decriminalization of abortions to the "worst enemy of the Greek nation" (Theofilos from Gortinia and Megalopoli, 1986) that stands against the truth and nature: "the tragedy of human liberty, the adventure of human failure," "the threat of the future of our race" (To Vima 3, 1985). It also equated mothers (instead of referring to them as women) with murderers ("Medeas") and identified abortions to the threat of extermination and war. In such cases, motherhood was aligned to nature, holiness, and blessing, while at the same time, the fetus appeared as a Greek citizen and sibling to (our national) family. Among anti-choice supporters, the supposed sympathy toward mothers produced an understanding of women who want to get an abortion as unstable and irrational. Within this discourse, women's subjectivity cannot be understood beyond "their mission": reproduction (Vradini 1, 1986).

Finally, primarily during 1985, articles appeared presenting lawyers' opinions toward the decriminalization of abortion. In these articles, the accountability justice shaped the concept of abortion as a complex legal issue which, on the one hand, provided women the ability and right to control an unwanted pregnancy but, on the other hand, worked against the problem of birth rate. In anti-choice legal arguments, the alignment of Greek society, nation, family, and individuals creates the "us" against women, and anti-abortion struggles are aligned with Greek patriotism and rationality (indicatively see Theoharatos, 1985; Ethnos 2, 1986; Ethnos 3, 1986; Vradini 3, 1986).

The analysis of the role of the press in the public debate about birth control in Greece was crucial for understanding the circulation of specific emotions and the alignments between different bodies of knowledge and notions that shaped the conceptualization of birth control and related issues. The press was also an essential source of publicity for the birth control debate, as those articles addressed Greek society as a general audience. Still, several questions remain: How did emotions work, and what bodies of knowledge were mobilized within the specific publics of the medical community, the political sphere, and the religious Press?

With regard to the medical community, a number of sources frame birth control through the concepts of abortion, contraception, and sterilization. These include archival sources such as medical textbooks, papers in scientific journals, conference proceedings, the Publication of the Greek Society for Family Planning, the magazine *Eleftho* (Association of Midwives of Attica), and the public statements of the Panhellenic Medical Association. A careful analysis of these materials shows that scientific knowledge in such discourses appears as unemotional, when in reality it is shaped by the circulation of fear directed at protecting the institution of the family.⁹ This is apparent in the definitions of the concept of contraception (temporary measures of preventing pregnancy) that are aligned with that of sterilization (permanent), abortions (ending an unwanted pregnancy), family planning (creation of a happy family), and control of reproduction. Love of family constructs ideas of women (alongside their needs and desires) as subjects that stand against the institution of family (family's needs or couple's needs). Love also defines the criteria for the classification of contraceptive methods (efficacy, dangers, reversibility, women's acceptance of the method), which are often aligned with either the problem of overpopulation or Greece's problem of low birth rate (indicatively, see Preveroudakis et al., 1980; Papanikolaou, 1986; Aravandinos, un.d.).

Furthermore, the feeling of care toward women operates as a discrimination mechanism. It relates the efficacy of the pill to a "normal sexual life," while it is considered less effective when women are mentally unstable due to casual sexual relationships (see Preveroudakis et al., 1980). Related correlations are apparent in the following: "IUDs and contraceptive pills require a normal sexual life while the use of contraceptive methods for casual or rare sexual relations can create psychological problems" (Preveroudakis et al., 1980). In such cases, contraceptive methods often appeared in relation to men's feelings ("men are under stress"; "Men face problems with ejaculation"; "Reduction of [men's] sexual pleasure and satisfaction," see Aravandinos un.d.). In many cases doctors present the different contraceptive methods (including Ogino Knaus, coitus interruptus, diaphragm, IUD, douches, pill, condoms, and breastfeeding) through a sense of neutrality, when in reality they do create a classification and allow women to feel fear and concern toward some of them. For instance, the unquestioned presence of breastfeeding as a contraceptive method occurs alongside the presentation of fifty-two side effects and contraindications of the pill. The IUD is described with a failure percentage instead of efficacy rates (Aravandinos, un.d.). In another case, contraceptive methods are classified as "traditional, mechanical, and modern" (see Sex Education, 1989).

In the case of the conceptualization of abortion, the supposed lack of emotion is translated into the direct classification of the practice of abortion, doctors, and women through language and terminology, thus circulating violence. More specifically, the medical community uses two different terms for abortion – *ektrosi* and *amvlosi*, through which they define *amvlosi* as the act of killing, taking the life of the fetus, performing a crime, and *ektrosi* as the procedure performed by doctors to end a pregnancy for medical reasons (indicatively see

---

⁹ The historical process of how scientific knowledge has been shaped as unemotional is beyond the scope of this manuscript. See Donna Haraway; Evelyn Fox Keller; etc.

Papanikolaou, 1987; Papanikolaou, 1987a; Sex Education, 1989). Abortion methods – *ektrosi* – include cervical dilation and curettage, vacuum aspiration, endometrial ablation, hysterectomy, the use of oxytocin, hypertonic saline instillation, and prostaglandin (Preveroudakis et al., 1980). On the contrary, abortion as amvlosi is presented as a dramatic condition that some women experience that is aligned with psychological, social, economic, and demographic complications and is conceptualized as a "social illness" and "epidemic" (Danezis, 1969). The anxiety over demographic decline circulates through a generalized feeling of panic that contradicts abortions to Greece's need to remain "powerful and viable geopolitically," lining it up with the fear "that our tribe will vanish" (Greek Society of Family Planning, un.d). This political management of the human body and life determines which subjectivities and reproductive choices fit and/or belong in the existing biopolitical order, producing at the same time specific forms of life, "the heterosexual, reproductive, gendered and national self" (Athanasiou 2014, p. 2, 2006. See also Deutscher, 2017).

Additionally, sterilization (as a method for controlling the size of the family) refers to the female-oriented methods of laparoscopy, colpotomy, and endoscopy. The supposed neutrality of scientific knowledge, in this case, classifies gendered bodies, aligning them to the limits of scientific research and the limits of bodies: the limited research in sterilization methods for men is presented as being due to scientific reasons, while the "more and easier points of intervention that the male" (see Preveroudakis et al., 1980).

The violence that circulates through language and the supposed lack of emotion in scientific knowledge results in another interesting division between sexuality and reproduction. This division appears between women as mothers and women who have aborted as sinners who hurt the institutions of marriage, family, and motherhood and need to be "scientifically educated and morally guided" (Louros, 1976). In such cases, (proper) women are considered with the "source of life," "the core of the family," and "society" and those that "shape human destiny" (see Vita, 1976).

The first official public statement by the Greek medical community on abortion decriminalization was in 1983 in the magazine *Medical Step*, marking a significant moment for birth control movements and signaling medical support for ending illegal abortions and breaking the silence. However, it is crucial to analyze their statement of support within the context of gender ideology in medical culture:

> the members of the Association do not aim to argue for or against abortions, while this issue concerns humans, their civilization, their consciousness,

society, and its moral and demographic parameters. They aim to argue against hypocrisy [...] regarding human pain [...]. We ask everybody to recognize the human drama that occurs [...], where life is in danger, and the State remains silent [...]. We ask for the formation of the law to stop human abasement, unfair guilt, and the illegal regime's bad conditions that affect women's health. We also ask for a time limit by which, besides the couple and the doctor (male/female), another voice is responsible for the decision regarding and the protection of the fetus. [...] We demand that Ministries of Health and Justice and all of the other relevant groups cooperate and contribute to the formation of a new law that will legalize abortions and protect the fetus. (Panhellenic Medical Association, 1983, my translation)

This quote discusses how doctors aim to establish boundaries between social and scientific realms to maintain neutrality as rationality. It supports abortion legalization but distances itself from women's struggles, framing abortion as a human issue rather than solely a women's issue. It uses neutral language to downplay the gendered aspect of (illegal) abortions and suggests the legalization of abortions with the protection of the fetus to balance the different opinions of the birth control debate.

As much as the medical community appears to construct bodies of rational-as-non-emotional knowledge, at the same time, the practice of production and circulation of knowledge within the community of doctors appears to be shaped mainly by fear, hesitation, and love (which are transformed into different kind of emotions). The political and regulatory spheres seem to follow the same process. In this case, I focus on four laws related to abortion and one related to family planning, alongside their Justification and Explanatory Reports and related discussion in parliament.

Hidden emotions that mobilized the regulations related to abortion in Greek legal history are closely attached to the nation and the institution of the family. Positive feelings toward abortion circulated alongside negative feelings and, thus, women who abort are mentioned in the first regulation that appeared in the Greek Penal Code (1834) under the Regency Council of Otto in Greece (LHP 1, 1835), according to which abortions (amvlosi) are punishable actions against the lives of others and considered homicides. Furthermore, it is stated that women, midwives, pharmacists, and other medical personnel "who do, indicate the way, and supply means to execute this crime." The second reference in the Greek legal history maintains the same frame and appears in the second Greek Penal Code – law 1492/1950 (LHP 14, 1950) (Crowned Democracy), where abortions (amvlosi) remain in the chapter about Crimes against life between homicides, suicides, and infant homicides. The law includes two articles, one that prohibits women from getting abortions through ektrosi or with other means and from killing the fetus in any way. Exceptions refer to health problems, rape, sexual harassment of underaged girls, the inability to resist, or incest. The second article refers to the prohibition of the circulation of any information about abortion. According to meetings in parliament between July 26 and 27, 1950 (LHP 2, 1950), legal abortions are characterized as "ethical or medical" while at the same time, arguments that support the flexibility of the law are guided by feelings of concern and care (of the State toward women), aligning the law to the modernization of the Greek penal code "according to the spirits and needs of contemporary society."

The following law was passed within the governance of New Democracy (LHP 12, 1978). Here, abortions (amvlosi) are framed as the "Removal or transplant of human biological substances" and, more specifically, the "Removal from alive people." The law now declares that "technical ektrosi" is allowed until the twentieth week in cases of fetus abnormalities or women's mental health issues. In parliament, arguments that both support and reject the law are motivated by love of the nation and the concern about demographic data. However, they are also aligned with the need to stop women's oppression, support women's equality, and protect motherhood, children, and families. Finally, they are aligned with homicides and acts that contradict "the natural and holy laws."

The law that decriminalizes abortions (1609/1986 (LHP 13, 1986)) is titled "Technical Termination of Pregnancy and Protection of Women's Health and other regulations, and it passed under the governance of the Panhellenic Socialist Movement." This law ensures women's access to medical clinics for the technical termination of pregnancies. It also guarantees the flow of information for avoiding unwanted pregnancies with scientific means and legalizes the termination of pregnancy with a woman's consent when it is performed by a professional team of physicians before the twelfth week, until the twenty-fourth week in cases of fetus abnormalities, or until the nineteenth week in cases of rape. Additionally, according to Article 5, for "the advertisement of means of technical termination of pregnancies," public circulation remains prohibited. However, abortions allowed when performed through family planning centers, referring to doctors and people involved in related practices, and when published in medical or pharmaceutical journals.

The discussions in parliament were long and tense, while both pro-choice and anti-choice supporters provided arguments and counterarguments for the content of this regulation. PASOK introduced the law to approach ethical, social, medical, and legal issues honestly and liberalize and modernize the related regulations. On the contrary, for arguments that denounce abortions completely, concerns over the crisis of "the moral world of [unprotected] women" align the law against the "national and moral bankruptcy of the government who actuate women to kill their children." At the same time, women are constructed as "heroine Greek mothers who always carry the responsibility of the children and the nation." The related explanatory report focuses on women's health, women's choice regarding motherhood, and the demolition of social inequalities. At the same time, in the justification report, it is evident that the government's idea to protect women is lined up with the circulation of scientific knowledge (see LHP 3, 1986; LHP 4, 1986; LHP 5, 1986; LHP 6, 1986; LHP 7, 1986; LHP 8, 1986; LHP 9, 1986).

While in Greece, there were two essential institutions of family planning, the law 1036/1980 titled "For Family Planning and Other Regulations" was vital as it indicated that (only) the State should be responsible for the education of experts and the circulation of related information to the public. Interestingly, the initial form of the law referred to the "education of intended spouses and married couples regarding issues of Genetics and Family Planning," and the language changed after Tsouderous' amendment (LHP 10, 1979). This law appears crucial for excluding women's organizations and associations from family planning services; from that moment, only the State and the medical community would be responsible for them[10].

Having in mind that religion and the Church have always had strong ties to the Greek State, played a crucial role in everyday life, and constitute essential elements of the Greek cultural landscape, it seems necessary to explore how and through which emotions bodies of knowledge regarding abortion and contraception were constructed in religious magazines and newspapers. Interestingly, concerning abortions, science appears to be the basis of the related arguments. Here, science was mobilized to show that abortions are not a scientific issue, but that the knowledge about them is still institutional and therefore trustworthy. This scientific body of knowledge was mobilized to demonstrate that the human fetus is "soul and body from the moment of the conception" (see Oi Filoi ton Polyteknon 1, 1983. See also, Oikogeneia, 1985; Akropolis 1, 1986). This argument was presented as a scientifically proven statement that was supported

---

[10] The two institutions for family planning in Greece were the Greek Society Family Planning and the Society for Family Planning. The former was founded on April 20, 1973, in Athens by volunteer doctors and academics due to their concerns regarding high abortion rates in Greece (Manidaki (2020) pp. 117–21). Of the thirty founding members, only four were women, and the administration comprised exclusively of men. The society admitted only experts as members and prioritized protecting marriage and family institutions; The Society of Family Planning was founded on November 25, 1976, initiated by Professor of Gynecology Kintis, who sought support from parliament member Tsouderou. Kintis emphasized women's education about contraception as the solution to abortion in Greece. Out of twenty-three founding members, fourteen were women, not all experts, spanning various social and political backgrounds. The society aimed to promote family planning and cooperated with the feminist birth control movement, providing information to all interested individuals (Manidaki, 2020, pp. 125–31).

by "specialized scientists" (i.e., biologists, doctors, teachers, lawyers) against "commercialized scientists" (Oi Filoi ton Polyteknon 2, 1983).

Within this frame, love of society and self support "true" science purporting that abortions are a criminal and harmful act. A characteristic example is the "infant homicide complex," according to which doctors, midwives, and women who are involved in abortions become "psychologically traumatized and have nightmares due to guilt and depression" (Oi Filoi ton Polyteknon 1, 1983). Love toward the fetus and thus life itself, as presented, aligned abortion with murder – infanticide and the nation's homicide, the Greek children's homicide – while the arguments linked it (the fetus) to nationalism and the famous slogan "Fatherland, Religion, Family." Here, the demographic problem was identified as the problem of ensuring Greek supremacy over the Turks. Abortion was aligned with contraception, prenatal testing, and euthanasia as a practice that should be prohibited in Greek society. Love was circulated as hate against women, establishing at the same time gender roles and normativity: "women are saved through procreation"; "deserters should be shot, and those who get or perform abortions are deserters of God's kingdom"; "motherhood is unquestioned in a real woman" (AD, 1978; Akropolis 3, 1986). The circulation of terror and hate was linked to the repeated reference to and screening of a highly inaccurate documentary called "Silent Scream" in many public spaces (including the parliament). This documentary was condemned by the medical community and viewed as means by which a doctor and anti-choice supporter "used the power of the image to prevent women from getting an abortion" (Oi Filoi ton Polyteknon 3, 1985; Akropolis 2, 1986).

I have analyzed the public presence of birth control in the press and the specific publics interested in birth control, such as the medical community, the political and governmental sphere, and the religious and more conservative press. I aimed to *catch* the *something* that women confronted through the affective epistemologies of *antimilima* – the different social realms or the publics where emotions circulated and surfaced individual and collective bodies of knowledge related to birth control, as Ahmed argues. The complex way that emotions did this in the press allowed different social groups to acquire access and visibility in the debate: journalists, women and feminists, the medical community, politicians, lawyers, and the opponents of birth control.

The access to the debate was quite open from individuals to groups, organizations, collectives, and institutions – whose power and popularity were significantly different. Along with their attachments and transformations, certain emotions bond with specific bodies of knowledge aligned with subjects, spaces, and concepts. This complex process conceptualized birth control in the press in a certain way. Put differently, it was the circulation of emotions that shaped the public birth control debate and those who had access to it as relevant groups while at the same time shaping the meaning of birth control and the concepts aligned with it.

The *who* and the *what* about birth control in Greece cannot be understood without the *how* and the *when*. In the press, most articles were published between 1983 and 1987. Fear bonded to women's health or the Greek nation. Love linked to the abstract concept of life, which women and knowledge related to birth control threatened. As the reaction against oppression and an effort to break the silence, anger circulated after the public statement of women who had aborted. Here, action as reaction to break the silence by mobilizing counter-action was reflected in the sheer number of articles published between 1983 and 1987 and the interrelationships between numerous publics.

Bodies of knowledge corresponding to the circulation of emotions in public debate politicized science. Abortion and contraception were portrayed as multi-faceted issues encompassing moral, legal, constitutional, political, scientific, and experiential dimensions rather than solely medical procedures. Emotional work, as well as work informed by emotions, established boundaries between these dimensions and detached the body of knowledge regarding birth control from its medical and scientific content. Politicization construed birth control as a social issue, but as the social was nonscientific, birth control was de-scienticized. In contrast, in Section 3 I will demonstrate how feminists constructed birth control as a social issue that *was* a scientific issue as well. This complex mechanism established another important boundary: how the division between emotion and reason that was performed in the debate in the press operated as a demarcation between science and society.

Most articles on abortion and contraception failed to emphasize science, resulting in a detachment from their scientific content, including scientific methods, practices, and research. This detachment influenced public debate, leading to polarization among social groups on issues such as pro-choice/anti-choice stances and opinions on contraceptive pills and legal reform. Consequently, women's experiences with different methods of contraception received minimal attention in press coverage. The discourse surrounding abortion and contraception, as mediated by newspapers and magazines, facilitated the public's engagement with these issues and extended an invitation to express opinions regarding these issues from moral, political, or ideological standpoints. However, this discourse relegated scientific aspects of the debate to the domain of experts, predominantly men. While fostering democratic participation, the discourse around abortion and contraception underscored the inherently undemocratic production and circulation of medical knowledge, thereby limiting women's involvement in these processes.

Put differently, democratization of the debate was conceptualized through gendered power relations and hierarchies of knowledge.

Emotions operated within institutionalized knowledge systems that traditionally prioritize rationality and objectivity. In the context of Greek constitutional history, abortion was initially considered to be a crime against life. It then became associated with the removal and transplant of human biological substances, and was ultimately framed in terms of women's health. *Amvolsi*, *ektrosi*, and the *technical termination of pregnancies* depict not only the alignment of certain bodies of knowledge but also the emotional conflicts that were happening outside such bodies of knowledge – within different social groups and multiple publics. Emotional narratives shaped by these laws positioned the State as the protector, the medical community as the implementer, and women as subjects in need. The regulatory focus was initially on the mother, then the pregnant woman, and ultimately women in general.

As in the legal public sphere, where legal-centered discourses were circulated, in the medical one, abortion was considered a political, social, moral, and legal issue that would balance politics, religion, patriarchy, and science. Silence, as a political choice (present in both legal and medical sources), did not counteract the decriminalization of abortion but ensured women's exclusion from the circulation of knowledge and the development of health policies. The linguistic division over abortion in medical textbooks was one of the many occasions through which emotions shaped scientific knowledge. The division between *ektrosi* and *amvlosi* was accompanied by methods, tools, and practices that referred only to *ektrosi*. This binary acquired a performative character that differentiated and classified the practice of abortion in terms of medical culture, devaluating the medical procedure of *amvlosi* and shaping medical culture. Contraception was communicated solely through isolated facts and absolute values, neglecting women's needs and experiences.

Religion groups and the Church mainly circulated terror and hate toward the government that passed the decriminalization bill and women who had aborted through discourses that shared love toward the Greek nation and the fetus that was perceived as a Greek citizen. Here, the concepts (abortions, women, the Greek state, and the fetus) were bonded with morality, gender performativity, and discrimination. Birth control was utterly detached from contraception since the latter was completely absent. But the absence of accessible information about contraception was identified as the communication of science without reproducing any scientific content. Through this absence (of scientific knowledge), such discourses shaped society's attitudes toward science and contributed to the hegemonization of narratives that constructed abortions as anti-patriotic-and-anti-feminine.

The multiple publics of birth control in Greece and their affective economies shape the *againstness* of the feminist affective epistemologies of *antimilima* – those who criticized the established emotional and epistemic regimes. At the same time, they position polarization that resulted in women's exclusion from knowledge production practices and the degradation of their experiences within the broader political culture of the polarization of (Greek) modernity, which is still visible in contemporary dipoles that emerge over critical social issues. Due to this polarization, the emotional was silenced as the experiential-and-the-non-scientific, while it was present and accumulated, and classified under the scientific-as-the-objective-and-rational. Due to this distinction, the boundary between science and society demarcated the relationship between the concept of birth control and the body, ensuring the distance between the two. It was due to the emotional work embedded in the birth control debate that specific ideas were attached to particular objects of knowledge – those that (re)produced gender power relations and women's oppression.

3 *Forness*: Sweaty Concepts and Women's Experiential Expertise

"We existed inside the broken mirrors of history [...]. You created the world [...]. You as humans, we as subhumans, you as powerful, we as weak, you, MEN with capital letters, women with small letters. You, with speech, we, with silence [...]. You, in politics, art, sex, we, with the cry, whisper, scream [...]. You, with memory, we, with oblivion. Your world is beautiful, isn't it? Your world is beautiful with such comfortable antinomies. Enough!" (Drakopoulou, 1980). Affective epistemologies of *antimilima* – subaltern knowledge systems that resist, revolt, and react – refer to women's experiential expertise developed within the various counterpublics of the feminist birth control movement. As affective epistemologies, they allow us to reapproach the relationship between emotions, experiences, and expertise, contributing to existing discourse (see Boddice, 2021, 2022). In the previous section, I demonstrated the role of emotion in the construction of boundaries, and in the production and circulation of knowledge between different social realms and institutional (or dominant forms of knowledge). Here, knowledges contested what Ahmed (2014, p. 170) calls "the rational as the unemotional." Now, I am interested in examining the development of women's and feminists' experiential expertise to show that affective epistemologies of *antimilima* contested the understanding of "the emotional and the unthought." It was precisely this critique that repositioned the epistemic value of experience.

Since its inception, the Greek feminist birth control movement has been supported both by women's organizations and associations (linked to political parties), as well as autonomous grassroots feminist groups (self-organized and independent political bodies), which hold different agendas and priorities but co-operated on multiple occasions. Created in those counterpublics, affective epistemologies of *antimilima* encompass the transgenerational gesture toward recognizing the blood, pain, fear, filth, shame, loneliness, discomfort, and nonconformism of the 300,000–500,000 illegal abortions that took place every year in Greece until their decriminalization in 1986. Affective epistemologies also embody women's bodily work of writing, reading, translating, thinking and feeling, theorizing, and organizing birth control practices that reflected local demands and needs and simultaneously informed international coalitions. This multileveled and (inter)national character of women's bodily work was affected by Greek students' or exiled intellectuals' return to Greece after the fall of the dictatorial regime (mainly from France and Italy) who carried their experiences from participation in international birth control movements. The constant presence of Greek feminist groups and organizations/associations also contributed to international networks and coalitions (i.e., Women's Reproductive Rights Campaign. See also Chordaki, 2024).

This bodily work generates a body of knowledges that creates a world that crumbles epistemic divisions. Affective epistemologies of *antimilima* is the experiential expertise treated as a *sweaty concept,* and as such, it consists of women's difficulty in creating space for experience and knowledge that did not fit in the existing social and epistemological order. Creating a symmetry between the past and the present, it contains my difficulty as a researcher in developing tools for the appropriate/effective analysis of such complex bodies of knowledge (see Chordaki, 2022a). In this way, (experiential expertise as a) *sweaty concept* is world-making and opens up in different past, current, and future possibilities of becoming, where collective structures of knowledge are produced by and produce experiences that transcend established taxonomies and enable *antimilima*.

Affective epistemologies of *antimilima* include issues related to communication practices, knowledge, material culture, spaces and networks, and the crucial role of ideology, gender, and sexuality in feminist practices of production and circulation of knowledge about abortion and contraception (see also Chordaki, 2023). I approach the feminist birth control movement as a boundary movement that operates both inside and outside the boundaries of science – in terms of knowledge, culture, practice, and institutions – in order to highlight the blurred boundaries between science and various publics. I also use the concept of counterpublics (women's and feminists' public spheres) to deconstruct the concept of the public sphere further, revealing its complexities and multiple layers – both in terms of the relationship between publics and counterpublics and those within counterpublics – focusing on the development of counter-discourses, rival forms of knowledge and counter expertise.

Counterpublics operate as the critique against the division between the private and the public. They emphasize the crucial role of publicization and the hybrid character of spaces and groups that, even though they were considered private (i.e., closed feminist groups), operated as public spaces in which women and feminists communicated knowledge about birth control. Similarly, the exploration of the concept of experiential expertise and its approach as a *sweaty concept* reveals the rich, often neglected, undoubtedly difficult to measure, and polymorphic nature of a type of expertise that is based on experience as women and feminists generate it. In this way, affective epistemologies of *antimilima* become a way to *exist* because they are ways of knowing – a type of knowing that is close to the skin. Skin as a surface full of footprints of affective rather than pathologized traumas produced by particular gender and power relations and of care generated within the feminist movement (see Avramopoulou, 2016). A feminist skin that is against and for – that allows and denies.

Affective epistemologies of *antimilima* were shaped within the local and international networks that depict national and transnational flows of knowledge through various mediums: publications, translations of books, international sources, local pamphlets, proclamations, posters, flyers, declarations, handwritten notes, and other forms of archival material (see Chordaki, 2022, 2023). Such media are employed for communication about birth control, emphasizing women's mutual self-education, the integration of medical knowledge with personal experiences, and the international exchange of information regarding organizational structures. Such archives include the Greek feminist and women's press, encompassing publications from both state-affiliated feminist organizations and autonomous groups, individuals, or editorial teams unaffiliated with any political entity. Within the comparative examination of these publications, I elucidate the distinctions between women's associations or organizations linked to political parties and autonomous women's movements, as delineated through their respective periodicals, and explore the nuanced interrelations within feminist counterpublics.

The feminist archives of affective epistemologies of *antimilima* include 10 publications of books, 50 pamphlets, leaflets, and so on, 26 Greek feminist and women's magazines, and 490 articles related to birth control.[11] Contributing to

---

[11] The Bulletin of Democratic Women's Movement, Logia tis Kinisis Dimokratikon Gynaikon Koukakiou, Sygchroni Gynaika, Anichto Parathyro, the Deltio Syndesmou Ellinidon Epistimonon, O Agonas tis Gynaikas, publication of the Association of Greek Housewives, publication of the Lyceum Club of Greek Women, Skoupa, I Poli ton Gynaikon, Katina, Gaia,

this archive are 51 local women's and feminist collectives and associations affiliated with Greek feminist birth control advocacy, engaged in circulating information regarding abortion and contraception; 40 international groups and organizations, comprising details concerning seven feminist periodicals originating from diverse nations, alongside 18 venues designated for women's and feminists' activities, and 140 events centered around birth control matters (for more see Chordaki & Stavridi, 2021, Chordaki, 2022).[12] These findings underscore the breadth of the feminist birth control movement within Greece and its integration into a broader international network aimed at knowledge exchange, with active participation from Greek women.

The multifaceted nature of science communication through which the experiential expertise was developed encompasses an array of activities including but not limited to publications, translations, exhibitions, and group formations. Additionally, women's knowledge was related to the establishment of organizations, performances and the orchestration of concerts, educational activities such as courses, conferences, meetings, and advocacy campaigns. Moreover, women built their expertise through public demonstrations, the creation of physical spaces and the dissemination of posters and magazines. At the same time, they were engaged in acts of solidarity, formulating memoranda, and establishing networks and communication channels. Here, the circulated knowledge was directed toward various stakeholders, including women, society at large, governmental bodies, scientific institutions, and healthcare systems. The overarching objective was to foster collaboration among individual women (including collectives, and organizations), midwives, and healthcare professionals. Such encounters would take place in hospitals, clinics, and information services (including media outlets), as well as family planning institutions, relevant ministries, and governmental authorities.

Within the context of feminist and women's press, discernible discrepancies and convergences emerge regarding the conceptualization, demands, and

---

Magazine of the Free Women's Movement, Publication for the Liberation of Women, Hypatia, Medusa, Sfynga, Anarhiko Enimerotiko Deltio, Periodiko Omadas Paremvasis Koufalion, To Milo kai to Fidi apo tin plevra tis Evas, the publication of Multi-National Women's Liberation Group, Telesia, Brotherhood of people from Kefalonia and Ithaki – Women's Group, Gynaikeioi Psithyroi, the publication of Women's Group in Law School, the publication of Greek Women from Northern Greece.

[12] For local and international groups and associations see the following: Movement for the Liberation of Women, Group of Sexuality and Contraception, Multi-National Women's Liberation Group, Women's Group of Self-Examination Amazones, Federation of Greek Women, Greek League for Women's, Union of Greek Women, Research Center for Information about Radical Fminism Feminaire, Women's Group in Boston, Union of Italian Women, West Auckland Community Health Group. For the venues see the following: Women's Station of Mutual Aid in Ampelokipoi, Women's Bookstore, Women's House in Athens.

implementation of birth control. Notably, women's associations and organizations linked to political parties predominantly directed their attention toward involvement in political spheres and the formulation of pertinent regulations, alongside advocating for state-regulated oversight of birth control, wherein they assert a participatory role while concurrently elevating the authority and expertise of professionals in this domain. They underscore the significance of the collaborative engagement of women in these endeavors to enhance institutional knowledge and practices. Conversely, autonomous movements and collectives prioritized self-organizational frameworks, interrogating the authority of experts and unveiling the ideological underpinnings inherent to scientific paradigms, methodologies, and cultural contexts. Their focus was cultivating their own systems of production and circulation of knowledge, relegating experts and state apparatuses to secondary roles. Central to their analysis is the conceptualization of experience, not as a supplemental facet within an established knowledge framework but as the primary wellspring from which they forge a novel paradigm, thereby challenging existing constructs. Regarding the different terms for abortion in the Greek language, most women and feminists use the term *ektrosi*, while the term *amvlosi* appears rarely and is used primarily by women's organizations (see Chordaki, 2023).

Within the feminist counterpublics, birth control was aligned with the concepts of abortion, contraception, sexuality, family planning, sex education, national and international events and activities, news and networks, feminist theory and theoretical approaches, the role of women in politics and their experiences and aimed, among others things, at limiting abortions through the simultaneous distribution of contraception.

For them, birth control is pivotal issue through which sexual intercourse is transformed into a human right, and personal experience evolves into a societal phenomenon with political ramifications. Furthermore, the alignment *abortion-contraception-sexuality*, as presented by the Autonomous Women's Movement, delineates birth control as an intrinsic women's right intertwined with self-determination. This association emphasizes responsiveness to women's needs and desires rather than demographic considerations or the preferences of male partners. Consequently, birth control reframes sexuality beyond reproduction, challenging the deterministic view of biology and anatomy. The "fundamental human-women's right" is thus identified as the self-determination of the body that laws and institutions cannot control, a right that can help women understand their sexuality apart from reproduction and the biological consequences of sexual intercourse. According to the Autonomous Women's Movement, historically, the natural reproductive ability of women has been a source of oppression and objectification, while the female body has been "hated, alienated and manipulated." Thus, they urge women to reject "anatomy as destiny" and work "separately and altogether" for the decriminalization of abortion, the spread of knowledge regarding contraception, and the right to sexual life: "If we, women, do not take the problem into our hands and fight for the solution, no one else will do it" (PACL 1, 1983).

As a hygiene-related concept, women's understanding of birth control opposes the naturalization of gender disparities, which perpetuate women's marginalization, subordination, and exclusion from societal, political, and scientific domains. Concurrently, birth control is interlinked with the redefinition of experiential concepts from a female perspective, underscoring women's struggle against hierarchical structures and prevailing social norms to assert their authenticity and worth. Related concepts such as orgasm are reconceptualized as mental and physical processes shaped by social factors and individual agency rather than mystique stemming from interpersonal dynamics (indicatively see Sfynga, 1980; Women's Collective & Malliakou, 1982). Masturbation is perceived as a means of bodily self-knowledge, while self-examination is viewed as an act dismantling the dichotomy between theory and practice, knowledge and expertise, while organs such as the vulva and clitoris are recognized as intricate components contributing to the experience of orgasm.

More specifically, in the Greek translation of the book *Woman and Her Body* (Women's Group in Denmark, 1980) the four stages of orgasm are presented as mental and physical processes, and the book describes the ways through which different reproductive organs respond to each stage, while they point out the importance of women's reconciliation with masturbation as a "mean for knowing their bodies and sexuality [...] establishing a relationship with the body, thinking of it, searching it, loving it" (p. 189). To that end, the book urges women to use a mirror to watch and explore their bodies and reproductive organs and feel free to choose how they will experience masturbation. In a related chapter, self-examination is also presented as both theoretical and practical. This chapter refers to the use of a dilator, which, alongside a mirror and a light, enables women to see their internal reproductive organs. The chapter provides a detailed description of what a woman might expect or should try to see: cervix and the uterus, the color, smell, and discharges which may indicate an infection, the phase of the menstrual cycle, the shape of the organs, the density and consistency of the mucus. Moreover, they urge women to keep notes of their observations. Similarly, they refer to breast self-examination, where women learn about their breasts and learn how to notice any changes.

Birth control aligned with the notion of abortion, which was perceived as a matter to be addressed through women's acquisition of pertinent knowledge and a medical procedure crucial for fostering equality and safeguarding women's rights. Historically, for women, birth control was viewed as an act of resistance, symbolizing women's active engagement in sexual activity – a manifestation of both vulnerability and empowerment – serving as a means to combat sexual exploitation and the oppression of female sexuality and bodies. According to women and feminists, reclaiming the body is akin to reclaiming the right to control their nature. In parallel, women and feminists also emphasize the importance of abortion in practice, which continues to happen throughout history despite laws criminalizing it. As they state, abortion is "the material basis of the possibility of women's resistance against the imposed limits of their role – that are based on reproduction." Instead of perceiving it as an abstract category, they (women and feminists) note that abortion was always a woman's way to participate in sexual intercourse through the safeguard pf a last-minute solution, "a type of resistance that comes through weakness and a lack of options [...], which embodies the coexistence of weakness and forcefulness" (DEC 2, 1983).

For them, abortion was depicted as an extreme form of contraception, countering prevalent beliefs portraying abortion as the predominant method of birth control in Greece. Decriminalization was perceived as a step toward increased visibility, public awareness, women's protection, preventive measures, and emergency recourse. A step against the illegal regime that was characterized by a fragmented service system, diminished emphasis on preventive medicine, the absence of robust health advocacy movements, an idealization of the medical profession – entailing power, authority, and a lucrative underground market – the limited circulation of knowledge, and prohibitive costs (Medusa 1, 1983).

Through this perspective, contraception, as an integral component of birth control, was characterized as a multifaceted issue encompassing medical terminology, social dimensions, and gender implications. Within feminist movements, contraception was advocated as a matter pertinent to all individuals regardless of gender, challenging the prevailing narrative that positioned contraception solely as a concern for women. Instead, it was portrayed as an intrinsic aspect of sexual activity, underscoring the pivotal role of individual attitudes toward contraception and its efficacy. Moreover, contraception was presented as intertwined with sexual liberation – a means for women to challenge perceptions of sex as a burdensome duty ("sex as a chore"), wherein they traditionally assumed a passive role. Its significance extended to the realms of health protection, self-awareness (facilitating bodily understanding), pregnancy prevention, and the enhancement of sexual experiences, countering narratives of sexual dissatisfaction.

Here, an essential aspect of women's struggle was to transform sex from a chore into an act of connection and communication (PACL 2; GIK, 1984) while finding means to fight sexual misery: "It is not our intention to substitute for doctors – we couldn't if we wanted to. However, basic knowledge will help us avoid fear, talk openly about our problems, and demand their solution. We call upon all those who are interested in our struggle [...] so that together, we may find other means of fighting sexual misery in our country" (DEC 1, 1977). Framed as both a women's right and a responsibility of the state, contraception was advocated for all individuals, spanning various stages of life from adolescence to menopause (BDMEDICALES, 2008). Women called for expanded scientific research and widespread promotion of contraceptive methods to combat societal hypocrisy and fight against silence.

In parallel, sexuality was communicated as a complex issue related to physical, mental, emotional, and political factors and as part of life, consequently affected by women's social position and their experiences of living in an androcentric society. It was approached as something that belongs to women rather than their lives in service of others. It was part of a political discourse through which women could abolish the consequences of biological difference and fight against the idealization of motherhood and the detestation of female bodies. It promoted the female gaze over feminine weakness central to dominant depictions of sexuality. In the book *For Ourselves. Our Bodies and Sexuality from Women's Point of View* (Meulenbelt, 1984), the author highlights the limits of language – a language that represents men and the medical community. She argues that women have not yet developed a dictionary that will be able to express their experiences and desires, while the dominant language about sexuality is either moral-centered or violent and scientific, and thus, it is a language that makes women feel their sexuality as something strange and distant. In that regard, she suggests (for a start) replacing the expression "I am coming to an orgasm" with the expression "I am doing orgasm" in order to convey that orgasm is not something that someone else gives us but rather an ability that is inside us – "a condition that we actively generate to ourselves" (p. 15).

Moreover, women's critique of the dominant view of sexuality was focused on its contradicted meanings – its parallel absence and idealization. In this ideology women appear to be creatures with no sexuality, and (their) sexuality itself is identified as dirt, immorality, sin, and prostitution. To that end, they (women and feminists) also criticized scientific approaches to sexuality, which perceive it as something that can be studied scientifically and measured with scientific instruments, excluding women's experiences, needs, and desires from the analysis. They write: "Women do not speak. They struggle to express themselves; there are no women's Logos, [women are often represented as] creatures without sexuality." Logos is defined as a "system of expression and communication: personal expression through verbal or written discourse, art, participation in science, and engagement with the public. The process of shaping the history of society, the ability to analyze and synthesize experience" (Medusa 2, 1983).

Furthermore, information about birth control was communicated through the concept of family planning, approached as a realm not exclusively under the purview experts, highlighting women's need to participate in such institutions. For women's associations and organizations linked to political parties, family planning was a concept related to family and society, while for autonomous movements it was associated with women's needs and desires. Thus, the concept was communicated through its correlation to women's emancipation, protection of their health, control of family and fertility, and responsible sexual relationships. In parallel, it was linked to the reorientation of the demographic problem and was presented as a measure for the prevention of sterilization, the improvement of women's sexual life and the distribution of responsibility to both partners. However, some autonomous groups conceived family planning as another aspect of the state's intervention in their lives and bodies.

Accordingly, sex education was communicated by autonomous groups as part of birth control that would encourage people to know their bodies. At the same time, it was conceived as an additional specialization for doctors and teachers that would help publics understand biological differences, reproduction, contraception, STDs, equality, gender roles, and the embodied ideology that is present in these concepts. Subsequently, birth control was communicated through the concept of motherhood that women redefined as a choice that the state should protect and a condition of gender equality that separates reproduction from family and acknowledges the parallel performativity of biological and social motherhood (indicatively see Pambouki, 1979; BDWM 1, 1981; BDWM 2, 1983).

The concept of birth control was also communicated through women's need to participate in politics to promote their needs and views and the institutional framing of gender and equality. Fighting against discrimination derived from the structures of the state, the legal system, and social prejudice, their participation in politics and decision-making promoted an alternative model for society and another type of political expression that would be achieved through the feminist political coalition (indicatively see Rapitou, 1981; Sygchroni Gynaika 60, 1985; Katina 3, 1987; Anichto Parathyro, 1988; Kotsovelou & Repousi, 1989).

Moreover, women and feminists themselves communicated the importance of experience and ideology in knowledge production, as well as the difficulty of expressing experiential discourse that enables the collective publicization of experience and detaches sensitivity from weakness and power from authority. They emphasize the crucial role of the communication of experience as something historical and social rather than a personal issue (see ASEPV 1, 1982; Gaia, 1983; Katina 2, 1988). Additionally, science is understood as a social activity that is related to capitalism, which cannot solve the problem of birth control technologically or independently from ideology and social relations. At the same time, women's participation in knowledge production and circulation is communicated as the right to produce discourses and question objectivity as the given a-historical and gender-neutral truth (Sfynga, 1980; Kourkoula, 1983; AIB, 1984).

I will now discuss the content of the produced and circulated knowledge to outline the concept of experiential expertise – the affective epistemologies of *antimilima*. This analysis will unfold along two concurrent axes: first, delineating the content of this knowledge; and second, establishing connections between this content and the societal requisites that precipitated the development of such knowledge and expertise. This expertise is rooted in women's lived epistemic, emotional, and sensorial experiences and is perpetually shaped through collaborative processes, interweaving with institutionalized forms of knowledge and expertise.

Women's and feminists' knowledge and expertise encompassed diverse subjects in a multidimensional framework that combines medical, social, and gendered perspectives. These subjects include but are not limited to: anatomical understanding, contraceptive methods, women's education regarding specific contraceptive implications and monitoring (i.e., diaphragm), alternative contraceptive methods (including nonpenetrative sexual practices), sterilization techniques, menstrual cycle management, abortion methods, bodily monitoring through sensory observation (including color, smell, density, discharges, mucus), physiological aspects, sexual fantasies, sexually transmitted diseases, circumcision, healthcare accessibility, menopause, breastfeeding, infertility, reproductive technologies, pregnancy, childbirth, medical instruments and devices, orgasm, sexuality, sexual relationships, and phenomena associated with anatomy, self-awareness, and forced sterilization.[13] These discussions include visual depictions of pertinent issues, redefinitions of associated

---

[13] Their analysis for contraceptive methods included: mechanisms, cost, user instructions, brand variations, side effects, contraindications, prerequisite medical examinations, practical advice, warnings, efficacy rates, expenses associated with medical consultations, associated risks, device size, materials, and prospects for future contraceptive technologies. For the abortion methods the discussion included considerations for evaluation based on women's experiences, potential complications, terminology, safety measures, pre-operative preparation, post-operative care, self-care protocols, early detection of conception, pregnancy testing, and self-examination practices.

concepts, realignment of experiential perspectives, and cultivation of various skill sets (see Chordaki, 2022).

Women and feminists focused on the inquiries a medical practitioner should pose to enhance the oversight of women's health, as well as the emotional states and experiences of women prior to, during, and after gynecological examinations and abortions. They also focused on methodologies to facilitate women's understanding of their bodies and underscored the significance of interpersonal dynamics, as well as societal and spousal attitudes toward contraception, in influencing the selection and effectiveness of contraceptive methods. Concurrently, they highlighted the allocation of responsibility for each contraceptive method and offered guidance on how couples could familiarize themselves with their chosen method. In tandem, they recounted women's experiences with various contraceptive methods during menstruation and shared insights on addressing specific complications and side effects associated with these methods. Moreover, they circulated legal knowledge, legislation particulars, and insights into local and international conditions, contexts, and experiences related to birth control. They focused on the role of their own knowledge and expertise in the education of experts, while at the same time, they emphasized the development of their own media, structures, the processes of establishing priorities in scientific research, and their correlation to power, social relations, and health care systems. Furthermore, their knowledge and expertise included issues related to the transformation of social relations among women themselves and men and women, as well as the structures of the state, politics, and science based on inclusion, diversity, freedom, equality, and equity.

Besides evaluating scientific knowledge, methods, and practices, women and feminists also proposed alternative approaches, definitions, and prioritization criteria. For example, regarding contraceptive methods, instead of the term "efficacy rates," women use the term "vulnerability," expressing their apprehension regarding the likelihood of an unplanned pregnancy and its associated risks (Women's Group in Denmark, 1980). Similarly, by criticizing the medical division of side effects into *soft* and *hard* or *critical* and *indifferent*, which results in the devaluation of the latter, they classify them based on their effects on particular organs, highlighting the significance of each side effect in women's daily lives (Women's Group in Denmark, 1980). At times, they substitute the term "contraception" with the expression "preventing pregnancy" and classify conventional contraceptive techniques labeled as "natural" under the category of "inadequate contraceptive methods" – recognizing that in Greece, alongside the prevalent use of abortions as a contraceptive measure, the withdrawal method emerged as one of the most widespread, yet ultimately ineffective, approaches (Meulenbelt, 1984, p. 271). Moreover, the evaluation of contraceptive methods is based on the alignment with women's preferences and requirements rather than their ethical implications.

This knowledge and expertise was intended for all women and intertwined with their relationships with their bodies and the female body's interactions with other women, men, doctors, the state, and institutional frameworks. Consequently, knowledge and expertise regarding birth control evolve into political matters. For example, the body, located at the core of their analysis, became a vehicle for political arguments aimed at women's liberation, empowerment, autonomy, and confidence. This perspective contrasts with narrow viewpoints that depict such knowledge as merely replacing expert opinions and undermining the credibility of scientific inquiry. It is pertinent to highlight that the body is not merely portrayed as an object of analysis and control but as an integral part of the analytical process – serving as a wellspring of knowledge actively involved in its production and circulation. Here, the body is reconfigured against the dominant ideology:

> We have been told that our bodies are ellipses in relation to the wholeness of the male body.
> Our bodies, as a bloody wound that bleeds every month due to her shame
> Our bodies as a black continent – inscrutable.
> Our bodies fragmented in posters
> An offer to their fantasies
> Our bodies as a commodity in the streets
> An offer in the kingdom of men and money

Our bodies have been recognized only when they embody another body. Recognition of our "surplus value." (Kiveli, 1979, my translation)

Nevertheless, what are the social needs that this feminist knowledge and expertise came to meet? Focusing on the co-productive role of ideology and political aims in knowledge production and circulation, I will show that the complexity of the social needs that resulted in the development of women's and feminists' knowledge and expertise was the core of rival content of the affective epistemologies of *antimilima*.

Affective epistemologies of *antimilima* were situated in women's social position and their firsthand encounters within an androcentric and heteronormative societal framework. The development of their own knowledge and expertise through the communication of birth control was an act of resistance to the dominant ideology, which was aligned with taboos, silence, myths, secrecy, and the refusal of the communication of knowledge. This ideology constructed women as objects, wives, and mothers and resulted in feelings of incompleteness, stress, detestation, guilt, loneliness, fear, shame, and insecurity. Their struggles thus aimed to challenge their hetero-determinism, the pervasive notion of their social inferiority, the perpetual expectation of sexual availability, the medicalization and stigmatization of their health concerns, the ideology of scientific objectivity privileging male perspectives, and the enduring mistreatment they suffered. Their knowledge and expertise emerged from a critique of the artificial division between emotion and orgasm, body and mind, the exclusive focus on male sexuality, the societal portrayal of women and their bodies as simultaneously enigmatic and debased ("mysterious and vulgar"), the reduction of female sexuality to reproductive functions, the link between sexual intercourse and power dynamics, and the authoritarianism within medical spheres that purportedly monopolized the truth. Their expertise was their discourse of resurrection:

> [Discourse of Resurrection is] a discourse, that despite the blanks, the spaces, the contradictions, and deficiencies, goes deeper and **touches the difficult, the one that hurts** [...]. **Despite the difficulty of being expressed, experiential discourse** provides a perspective of our reality, not only with the things we say but also with those **left unsaid**. There is a functionality in these women's discussions. It is the **collective publicization** of our guilt, the exploration of the reasons for our problems and desires [...] What we want is not the production of theory but **a way to change our lives,** and to change it, we need to **know** our lives through the multiple reflections that are come into sight daily from every direction and are presented as "our lives [...]. We need to find, in each and every moment, the point where **sensitivity** will not be weakness and power will not be authority [...]. This **is women's way** [...]. Women's groups are ways to explore the relationship between us [...] and move forward through them with **warmth and humanity**. We express ourselves **freely** [...], with love and security [...]. We feel closer to each other; we act **spontaneously**; we create [...]. How can we **transfer** these experiences to other parts of our daily lives? [...]. Feminism is not just another activity but **a life matter** (CSHA, my emphasis and translation).

Women need to question and fight against the hierarchical society and relationships that oppress them while regulations simply represent a "social reality." Analyzing issues related to prejudice, sexuality, family, work, prison, school, and house, in another article, they discuss the correlation between health, nutrition, abortion, contraception, medication, and nuclear energy, noting that regulations about abortions are in fact regulations about the "ownership of the female body." For them, the slogan "the personal is political" is identified with the politicization of experience and allows women to fight against the "monopoly of certain types of knowledge and information" by developing and establishing "new experiences" (I Poli ton Gynaikon). To understand these experiences, they need to reconfigure the concept of experience and body, the social position of women in Western societies, and feminist practices. Practices that were developed within the closed feminist groups where women's exclusive presence allows them to discover their "authenticity," reestablish relationships with other women, and "value their own existence" and translate this experience and knowledge "of being a woman within the social reality."

Such knowledge is identified with women's experience of their position in society by emphasizing the feeling of exclusion in a "society which is dominated by male desire and models and where being a woman with women's experience and desires is something that does not fit in." Central to this is the role of the body – "'which is at stake' – and women's difficulty in being part of society, which 'makes her feel like a stranger in a world that she does not belong to.' [...]. Thus, they demand more space within a society that does not value equality." To connect with each other means to create a familiar world for women, "while in this world, from the factory to the laboratory, from the kindergarten to sports areas; from the law to poetry, it is the dominance of the male body which is constantly applauded." What they mean by the familiar world for women is a "network of relationships, in which we will be able to record and make efficient our experiences, collecting and developing a practical knowledge that women have acquired through difficult situations that they have been through. In other words, we should develop ways to exist in the world and at the same time to improve the relationships between us" (Katina 1, vol. 7).

Women and feminists responded against limited scientific research, widespread unawareness, and the dominance of hard rationality over fantasy. At the same time, they criticized doctors' attitudes against women's involvement in the production and circulation of knowledge, alongside the naturalized identification of sex with pain and the consideration of their experiences as false and irrelevant. Such attitudes were accompanied by doctors' sabotage of contraception and the role of antagonism in knowledge production. Additionally, they were situated in the effects of women's dependency on doctors and their heroization, the fragmentation of the human body, the promotion of medication as a "magic panacea," the devaluation of women's symptoms, needs, and desires, the paternalistic approaches, women's exploitation, the circulation of misinformation and distorted images concerning birth control, men's perception of contraception as a mean that is defined as women's sexual availability, women's humiliation, patronization, and misery (indicatively, see Boston Women's Health Book Collective, 1984).

This knowledge and expertise sought to empower women by instilling confidence, enabling them to question scientific authority, exposing the dominant ideologies surrounding birth control, emphasizing preventive measures and prompt treatment, fostering a sense of responsibility for their own bodies, reclaiming autonomy and control, developing a language rooted in personal experiences, and enhancing their ability to perceive and understand their bodies. Self-determination constituted a central focus of their analysis, while concurrently, their knowledge and expertise were founded on the incorporation of diverse perspectives, opinions, and experiences, as well as the cultivation of trustworthy relationships with experts (see indicatively Crinon, Manes et al., 1979; Chordaki, 2020).

Affective epistemologies of *antimilima* show how it feels to have the need to produce and circulate knowledge in a world that took your right to do so and how it feels to relate your different types of knowledge with science – when the latter does not accept anything different. Most importantly, it shows the weight of such questions in the context of threat. The threat not only of being emotionally and epistemically isolated but also physically tortured in a basement, on a wooden door used as an operating table (see Ta Nea 2, 1976). This is what creates a precise alignment or symmetry between emotions, rationality, and the body creating at the same time an act of resistance – a space and a breath. This is the process of making *sense* of knowledge.

Affective epistemologies of *antimilima* comprise a comprehensive body of knowledge characterized by its concreteness, holism, multilayered nature, steadfastness, communicability, multidirectionality, contextual relevance, democratic ethos, political significance, and resistance. Within this framework, numerous contradictions emerge, revealing the inherent complexities of dichotomous ideologies and their pivotal role in shaping knowledge production and circulation: this framework embodies traits of both weakness and strength, academic rigor and vulgarity, solidity and fluidity, technical/scientific/practical aspects alongside emotional/imaginative/utopian dimensions, situatedness and embodiment, abstraction and definition, clarity and complexity, and connections to memory, intergenerational sentiments and experiences, trauma, pain, and isolation, as well as bodily fluids such as sweat, blood, and discharges.

It (affective epistemologies) is a phenomenon deeply rooted in and directed toward the body, conceptualized as a nexus intersecting the material, ideological, social, relational, and gendered dimensions of existence rather than merely a physical structure composed of bones, organs, and skin. Experiential expertise within this paradigm is collaboratively cultivated through practices of knowledge circulation, the establishment of local and international networks, mutual exchange and education, and the transformation of personal/private/local narratives into public/collective/international spheres. It involves the recognition, documentation, and sharing of experiences as well as the reinterpretation of these experiences through communication. It also fosters collaboration with experts, and envisions alternative realities for women and their women's aspirations about their bodies, lives, capacities, experiences, scientific engagement, and citizenship.

Treating experiential expertise of women and feminists of the Greek birth control movement as a *sweaty concept*, the notion answers questions regarding specific meanings, ideologies, and social groups represented by the dominant language and terminology related to birth control's exclusion of others. It asks questions about the social factors that affect knowledge production and circulation, while at the same time, it discusses the role of social factors in women's perception of their bodies and sexualities. It focuses on establishing trustworthy relations with experts and developing feminist pedagogies to share knowledge. It is the emotional work needed to rationalize women's experiences of certain phenomena that aims to liberate them and their sexuality. It is the rational-as-emotional work needed to create a language that can move between senses and thoughts. It is necessary to continuously ask what the sources of knowledge are instead of stabilizing the answer to this question.

Affective epistemologies of *antimilima* are the set of questions needed to explore the concept of experiential expertise in the history of the Greek birth control movement, where experience reorganized the classification between emotion and reason and the reconfiguration of the relationship between the rational and the emotional prioritized experience, reclaiming its epistemic value. Thus, experience, gender, and science as interrelated concepts produced the situated concept of birth control in the first decades after the fall of the dictatorial regime in Greece.

Conclusions: Making *Sense*

"Your life proves that we are not what we do, but rather that we are what we haven't done, because the world, or society stood in our way. [...] The history of your suffering bears these names. Your life story is the history of one person after another beating you down. The history of your body is the history of these names, one after another, destroying you. The history of your body stands as an accusation against political history." (Louis, 2018, p. 27, 79) Talking back is an act that reorganizes our relationship with time and, hence, our perception of history. Talking back provides new possibilities to reconstruct our histories – those histories that are situated in the past but are regenerated by the histories of our present. Making *sense* of knowledge is the feminist struggle to develop affective epistemologies of *antimilima*. It describes how Greek women and feminists of the late twentieth century politically negotiated the epistemic relationship between institutional and extitutional forms of knowledges, centralizing the role of the body. However, to understand this negotiation deeply, one needs to renegotiate this complex relationship in the present. In that sense, making *sense* of knowledge is also the theoretical-as-political journey that

I experienced while navigating the challenges of the past negotiations. This includes the difficulties I faced while I was trying to locate, approach, think, and theorize such negotiations. While I was studying the travel of knowledge in different epistemic and social realms as they appeared in the Greek feminist birth control movement, the knowledge I produced traveled itself in multiple disciplinary and political realms. While I was trying to understand what exactly it meant and how it felt for the women and feminists of the era of Metapolitefsi to fight against the epistemic, social, and gender order to protect themselves from the violence of not fitting in, I was in parallel trying to create a safe place for those histories to fit in.

In that sense, this history is not a past history or the description of a history of the past, but the archive that historicizes the multiple ways and manifestations of how it feels to be a feminist and experience reproductive and gender injustice, epistemic discrimination and biopolitical disciplinization. These past, present, and future struggles describe, as Ahmed notices, the emotional work needed to bring theory home – to reclaim. The emotional work. Because in feminist struggles, bringing theory home is an act of resistance, an act of survival and a way to imagine. These struggles sometimes feel cold and lonely, have the taste of the blood and the pain of the thousands of women who suffered and continue to suffer from illegal abortions, and depict the fear of others who do not have access to reproductive and sexual health services or are victims of forced sterilization. These struggles show that theory and our relationship to theory can also be a way to survive. To connect your body to theory and produce theory with your body can be a way to exist, breathe, and live. Here, the body as the corporeal, social, and political body – the individual as the collective body, the body that feels – brings theory home by transforming it into a home. In that sense, this history shows the emotional aspect of the knowledge aspect of body politics. It is a way to uncover to recover. At the same time, the act of intervention itself that is embodied in these struggles creates a utopian space, an imaginary place, or a different future. In that sense, these struggles feel warm. The warmth of connection, the sweet taste of the transformation of vulnerability into a mechanism of bonding, the sense of liberation that comes with breathing, the love felt when one collectivizes their individual experiences.

Experience was a central concept and analytical category in this study. It was crucial not only as a source of knowledge that derives from and is directed to bodies but also as the epistemological angle necessary to transform past and future experiences by reclaiming the relationship to knowledge. This process, as emotional, sensorial, and rational, allowed me to show the struggles to renegotiate the epistemic status of experience and, thus, intervene in the given classifications. Through the affective economies of the birth control debate – the complex ways through which emotions worked in relation to the knowledge produced regarding birth control – I showed how their circulation within the publics (the press, the legal/constitutional and medical communities, and the para ecclesiastical and religious press and publications) aligned social groups, communities, specific conceptualizations and forms of knowledges against others and established sharp boundaries.

As I have discussed here, it was not that the hierarchies of certain emotions created hierarchies between certain subjects and knowledges, but rather it was the different objects and bodies upon which certain emotions were attached that led to different alignments, which in turn produced certain classifications. Moreover, the circulation of emotions in the birth control debate showed not only the tensions between pro-choice and anti-choice supporters but also those between pro-choice supporters, the category of women as constructed by them, and knowledge. In this case, the analysis of the affective economies of the debate revealed how the differences in the ideologies and argumentations between pro-choice and anti-choice supporters dulled if we focus on the classification of experience and the construction of the subject of women. As I have shown, even in the case of pro-choice supporters (as they appear in different publics) women often were constructed as the vulnerable subjects that needed the help and protection not only of a paternalistic state but also of scientific knowledge. Put differently, despite different alignments of emotions, the State appeared as the protector, the medical community as the implementer, and woman as a subject in need. However, emotions played another crucial role in the debate. As I have argued, they resulted in the politicization of science, transforming birth control into (a problematic perception of what is considered as) a social issue.

Nevertheless, here, the social was constructed as the nonscientific, and thus, birth control was de-scienticized and moralized. Despite the presence of multiple alignments and counteralignments, it was the division between emotion and reason that resulted in the sharp demarcation between science and society. This division also resulted in the polarization of the debate that led to women's exclusion from knowledge related to birth control, and the direct link between birth control and scientific knowledge that degraded experience in the existing epistemological classification. Such exchanges between the different forms of knowledge and their different relations to experience were emotional. Here, established forms of knowledge such as the scientific, the constitutional, or even their interrelations, classified experience, and this classification of experience and affect as the nonrational reassured in return the dominance of those specific forms of knowledge.

The *againstness* of the affective epistemologies of *antimilima* was the *againstness* of these established epistemic and emotional regimes, and the latter took place in feminist counterpublics, as they were shaped between autonomous feminists and women's associations and organizations linked to political parties. Here, I focused on the production and circulation of knowledge and expertise from women and feminists within the feminist birth control movement as acts of *forness*. I have argued that the affective epistemologies of *antimilima* were feminist contestations of the rational as unemotional as well as critiques repositioning the epistemic value of the experience. I have described the affective epistemologies of *antimilima* as the bodily work needed to generate bodies of knowledge that create a world that crumbles epistemic divisions. And as such they also allow us to imagine a world understood and constructed beyond the ideology of division that produces the other. They are *for* this world. Here, knowledges and experiences are co-produced to transcend taxonomies and enable *antimilima*. These practices often need the development of reverse alignments – processes to deconstruct the dominant alignments coming from hegemonic publics. Affective epistemologies of *antimilima* show that our relationship to knowledge is a matter of life and death and an act of survival. Here, my focus on experience reorganizes the classification between emotion and reason as a response against oppression. Indeed, affective epistemologies of antimilima are a response against, but they are also the question for. In that sense, they demand to continuously ask and never stabilize the answer to the question of the sources of knowledge. Sources of knowledge can be a chance to breathe. Affective epistemologies of *antimilima* were developed by women's and feminists' sweat rather than divisions. A sweat that comes from fear, difficulty, passion. The bodies that sweat are situated bodies that are both the subject and the object of knowledge and expertise – of the affective epistemologies of *antimilima*.

I have identified the feminist birth control movement as the struggle for women's survival and a call for the democratization of both science and society in general. As a fight against patriarchy, it was a struggle for equality, self-control of reproductivity, self-determination, women's independence, sexual liberation, and reclaiming their bodies. I have showed that reclaiming their bodies meant for women to reclaim knowledge, and reclaiming knowledge meant to deconstruct the division between emotion and reason. For them, the concept of birth control included the methods for the prevention of pregnancy, their reproductive rights, the ability to have a healthy sexual life, and their access to knowledge and medical treatments. Here, I have shown the critical role of knowledge/expertise – as it was conceptualized by women and feminists – in reproductive justice. The access to and the control of knowledge. For the feminist birth control movement, birth control was reconceptualized as a social issue because it was a scientific one – a medical act.

This is an account of how epistemic decolonization can trouble History. An account that can contribute to the historiography of Metapolitefsi by opening up a dialogue with the historiography of the era of the democratic transitions in post-dictatorship European countries. It shows how a political history can be informed by histories of knowledge and epistemologies, transforming social movements from movements related to political rights to movements related to knowledge production as a political act. It also shows the political importance of epistemological classifications and the division between emotion and reason, and it reconstructs worlds that fit histories that do not fit in the existing order. Affective epistemologies of *antimilima* produced relationalities between the body, the world, and theory, while at the same time, they reoriented the status of knowledge and experience. They are the proof of experiences of survival even if their subjects and their histories were not expected to survive. They can be the scars in the name of love and protection. They are shaped not only by limits but also by possibilities. They were constructed not only by traumas but also by care. Hence, the history of affective epistemologies of *antimilima* is the history of the injustice that leads us to past histories of injustices in order to produce histories of justice. Affective epistemologies situate women's struggles of the twentieth century to the political demands and commitments of today's struggles. The contemporary struggle to grapple with the history of being woman – or fighting as Edouard Louis writes for the right to be a woman (2022) – not as an essentialist category but as a radical identity of resistance. Affective epistemologies of antimilima shape how those of us who identify as women make *sense* of the world around us as it is shaped through the process of making *sense*.

References

AD: Vasilopoulos, H. (1978). *Why Do Abortions belong to the Sins that Are Related to the Hands*. File 7A. ΟΠΕ [Απόσπασμα βιβλίου: Η έκτρωση ανήκει στα αμαρτήματα των χεριών].

Ahmed, S. (2004). *The Cultural Politics of Emotion*. Edinburgh: Edinburgh University Press.

Ahmed, S. (2010). *The Promise of Happiness*. Durham: Duke University Press.

Ahmed, S. (2014). *Willful Subjects*. Durham: Duke University Press.

Ahmed, S. (2017). *Living a Feminist Life*. Durham: Duke University Press.

Ahmed, S. (2018). Συν-αισθηματικές Οικονομίες [Affective Economies]. In E. Avramopoulou, ed., and O. Tsiakalou, transl. *Το συν-αίσθημα στο πολιτικό. Υποκειμενικότητες, εξουσίες και ανισότητες στον σύγχρονο κόσμο*. Athens: Nisos, pp. 129–168. (In Greek)

Ahmed, S. (2018a). Αλλάζοντας χέρια. Μερικές σκέψεις για το *Sex, Gender and Society* της Ann Oakley. (Trans. by O. Tsiakalou). *Feministiqa*, 1. https://feministiqa.net/allazontas-cheria-sex-gender-society-ann-oakley/ [Accessed 3 March 2024].

AIB: Unknown Author (1984). Birth Control – Abortions. *Anarhiko Enimerotiko Deltio*. [Έλεγχος γεννήσεων – εκτρώσεις. Αναρχικό Ενημερωτικό Δελτίο].

Akropolis 1: Unknown Author (1986). The Crusade of Abortions Is Spreading. *Akropolis* [Απλώνεται η σταυροφορία κατά των εκτρώσεων. Ακρόπολις].

Akropolis 2: Unknown Author (1986, April 6). The Reactions Regarding Abortions Are Getting Bigger. *Akropolis*. [Διογκώνονται οι αντιδράσεις για τη νομιμοποίηση των αμβλώσεων. Ακρόπολις].

Akropolis 3: Unknown Author (1986, March 23). More Attention. *Akropolis*. [Περισσότερη προσοχή. Ακρόπολις].

Anichto Parathyro: Unknown Author (1988, vol. 42). Section Activities. *Anichto Parathyro*. [Δραστηριότητες. Ανοιχτό Παράθυρο].

Apolopoulou, M. (1986, July). Yes, in Abortions with the Parallel Prioritization of Contraception. *Nea Oikologia*. [Ναι στις αμβλώσεις προτεραιότητα στην αντισύλληψη. Νέα Οικολογία].

Apogevmatini 1: Unknown Author (1986, January 26). The Attack against Margaret. *Apogevmatini*. [Επίθεση κατά Μάργκαρετ. Απογευματινή].

Apogevmatini 2: Unknown Author (1986, January 31). Abortions Are a Premeditated Murder. *Apogevmatini*. [Φόνο εκ προμελέτης αποτελούν οι εκτρώσεις. Απογευματινή].

References

Apogevmatini Kyriakis: Unknown Author (1986, January 26). Margaret Is Accused. *Apogevmatini Kyriakis*. [Η Μάργκαρετ κατηγορείται. Απογευματινή Κυριακής].

Aravandinos, D. I. (Unknown Date). *Physiology of Woman*. Athens: Scientific Publication Gr. Parisianos. [Φυσιολογία της γυναίκας].

ASEPV: Unknown Author (1982, vol. 2). Feminism and Ecology. *To Milo kai to Fidi apo tin plevra tis Evas*. [Φεμινισμός και Οικολογία. Το μήλο και το φίδι από την σκοπιά της Εύας].

Athanasiou, A. (2001) *Nostalgic Futures, Contentious Technologies: Reckoning Time and Population in Greece*. Unpublished PhD Thesis. New York: New School University.

Athanasiou, A. (2006). Bloodlines: Performing the Body of the "Demos," Reckoning the Time of the "Ethnos." *Journal of Modern Greek Studies*, 24, 229–56.

Athanasiou, A. (2014). Το εθνικό σώμα σε κατάσταση έκτακτης ανάγκης: Η δημογραφική πολιτική της ζωής και τα όρια του πολιτικού. In E. Papataxiarhis, E. Plexousaki, K. Rozakou, and G. Giannitsiotis, eds., Αναθεωρήσεις του Πολιτικού: Ανθρωπολογική και Ιστορική Έρευνα στην Ελληνική Κοινωνία. Athens: Alexandreia, pp. 455–85.

Athanasiou, A. (2017). *Agonistic Mourning: Political Dissidence and the Women in Black*. Edinburgh: Edinburgh University Press.

Athanasiou, A. (2018). Το να "γίνεσαι φεμινίστρια" ως κριτική επιτελεστηκότητα του πολιτικού. In Nt. Vaiou and A. Psarra, eds., *Εννοιολογήσεις και πρακτικές του φεμινισμού. Μεταπολίτευση και «μετά»*. Athens: Workshop Proceedings. The Hellenic Parliament Foundation for Parliamentarism and Democracy, pp. 19–33.

Athanasiou, A. (2020, Autumn). Θεωρία φτιαγμένη από ιδρώτα. *Feministiqa*, 3. https://feministiqa.net/theoria-ftiagmenh-apo-idrwta/ [Accessed 28 September 2023].

Athanasiou, A. (2023, April 3). Πέντε χρόνια φεμινιστιqά/feministiqa: Το περιοδικό ως φόρουμ κριτικής δημοσιότητας μεταξύ έρευνας και ακτιβισμού [5 Years Feministiqa: The Magazine as Forum of Critical Publicity between Research and Activism]. Online Seminar with E. Avramopoulou, M. Liapi, E. Tzelepis. Online Seminar Series Εθνογραφείν Δημόσια ανθρωπολογία, Θηλυκότητες, Ανδρισμοί και Φεμινιστική Κριτική [Ethnografin]. (In Greek).

Athanasiou, A. & Tzelepis E. (2010). Thinking Difference as Different Thinking in Luce Irigaray's Deconstructive Genealogies. In A. Athanasiou and E. Tzelepis, eds., *Rewriting Difference: Luce Irigaray and "the Greeks."* Albany: State University of New York Press, pp. 1–14.

Avdela, E. & Psarra, A. (1985). Ο φεμινισμός στην Ελλάδα του Μεσοπολέμου: μία ανθολογία [Feminism in Greece during the Interwar Period: An Anhtology]. Athens: Gnosi.

Avdela, E., Papagiannaki, M., & Sklaveniti, K. (1986). Έκτρωση 1976–1986. Το χρονικό μιας διεκδίκησης. *Dini Feminist Magazine*,1, 4–29.

Avgeridis, M., Gazi, F., & Kornetis, K. (2015). Εισαγωγή. In M. Avgeridis, E. Gazi, K. Kornetis, eds., *Μεταπολίτευση. Η Ελλάδα στο μεταίχμιο των δύο αιώνων*. Athens: Themelio, pp. 9–26.

Avgi: Unknown Author (1986, January 21). Crusader. *Avgi*. [Σταυροφόρος. Αυγή].

Avramopoulou, E. (2016). The Affective Echoes of an Overwhelming Life: The Demand for Legal Recognition and the Vicious Circle of Desire in the Case of Queer Activism in Istanbul. In O. Alexandrakis, ed., *Impulse to Act: A New Antrhopology of Resistance and Social Justice*. Bloomington: Indiana University Press, pp. 41–62.

Avramopoulou, E. (2017). Hope as a Performative Affect: Feminist Struggles against Death and Violence. *Subjectivity*, 10, 276–93.

Avramopoulou, E., ed. (2018). *Το Συν-αίσθημα στο Πολιτικό. Υποκειμενικότητες, Εξουσίες και Ανισότητες στον Σύγχρονο Κόσμο*. Athens: Nissos.

Avriani: Unknown Author (1986, January 1). Sartzetakis, Andreas and Serafim Agree According to Psaroudakis. *Avriani*. [Σαρτζετάκης, Ανδρέας και Σεραφείμ συμφωνούν λέει ο Ν. Ψαρουδάκης και διαψεύδει την καθημερινή. Αυριανή].

Azocar, M. J. & Ferree M. M. (2016). Engendering the Sociology of Expertise. *Sociology Compass*, 10, 1079–89.

BDMEDICALES. (2008). *Clémentine ou la contraception*, www.bdmedicales.com/albums/clementine-ou-la-contraception.htm.

BDWM 1: Unknown Author (1981, vol. 19). Sex Education at Schools. *Deltio Kinisis Dimokratikon Gynaikon*. [Σεξουαλική Αγωγή στα σχολεία. Δελτίο Κίνησης Δημοκρατικών Γυναικών].

BDWM 2: Unknown Author (1983, vol. 11). The Necessity of Sex Education. *Deltio Syndesmou Ellinidon Epistimonon*. [Η αναγκαιότητα της σεξουαλικής αγωγής. Δελτίο Κίνησης Δημοκρατικών Γυναικών].

Bensaude-Vincent, B. (2009). A Historical Perspective on Science and Its "Others." *Isis*, 100, 359–68.

Benson, R. (2009). Shaping the Public Sphere: Habermas and beyond. *American Sociologist*, 40, 175–97.

Berlant, L. (2022). *On the Inconvenience of Other People*. Durham: Duke University Press.

Bioubi, F. (1976, May 23). Sixteen Years since the Circulation of the Pill. Miracle or Curse? *To Vima tis Kyriakis*. [16 χρόνια από την κυκλοφορία του χαπιού. Θαύμα ή κατάρα; Το Βήμα της Κυριακής].

Blume, S. (2016). In Search of Experiential Knowledge. *Innovation: The European Journal of Social Science Research*, 1–13.

Boddice, R. (2021). *Humane Professions: The Defense of Experimental Medicine, 1876–1914*. Cambridge: Cambridge University Press.

Boddice, R. (2022). *Scientific and Medical Knowledge Production, 1796–1918: Experiment, Expertise, Experience*, 4 volumes. Abingdon, Oxfordshire: Routledge.

Boddice, R. & Smith, M. (2020) *Emotion, Sense, Experience*. Cambridge: Cambridge University Press (Elements in Histories of Emotions and the Senses).

Borkman, T. (1976). Experiential Knowledge: A New Concept for the Analysis of Self-Help Groups. *Social Service Review*, 445–56.

Boston Women's Health Book Collective (1984 [1979]). M. Magganari (Transl.), M. Mitsou – Pappa (Ed.), *Our Bodies, Our Selves*. Athens: Ipodomi. [Ομάδα Γυναικών Βοστώνης. Εμείς και το σώμα μας].

Brito, M. V. (2020). Representing Silence in Politics. *American Political Science Review*, 114(4), 976–88.

Brito, M. V. (2020a). Silence in Political Theory and Practice. *Critical Review of International Social and Political Philosophy*. https://doi.org/10.1080/13698230.2020.1796328.

Brito, M. V., Jung T., Gray S., & Rollo T. (2019). Critical Exchange: The Nature of Silence and Its Democratic Possibilities. *Contemporary Political Theory*, 18(3), 424–47.

Brown, P., Zavestoski, S., McCormick, S., et al. (2004). Embodied Health Movements: New Approaches to Social Movements in Health. *Sociology of Health & Illness*, 26, 50–80.

Brown, W. (2001). *Politics out of History*. Princeton: Princeton University Press.

Browne, V. (2014). *Feminism, Time, and Nonlinear History*. New York: Palgrave MacMillan New York.

Butler, J. (1993). Imitation and Gender Insubordination. In H. Abelove, M. A. Barale and D. M. Halperin, eds., *The Lesbian and Gay Studies Reader*. New York: Routledge, pp. 307–20.

Castro, M. E., Van Regenmortel, T., Sermeus, W., & Vanhaecht, K. (2019). Patients' Experiential Knowledge and Expertise in Health Care: A Hybrid Concept Analysis. *Social Theory and Health*, 17(3), 307–30. https://doi.org/10.1057/s41285-018-0081-6.

Catalog. (2005). *Ο φεμινισμός στα χρόνια της μεταπολίτευσης 1974–1990. Ιδέες, συλλογικότητες, διεκδικήσεις*. The Hellenic Parliament Foundation. For Parliamentarism and Democracy, Athens.

Chalkia, A. (2007). *Το άδειο λίκνο της δημοκρατίας. Σεξ, έκτρωση και εθνικισμός στην σύγχρονη Ελλάδα*. M. Kastanara (Transl.) and Ch. Konstantaki, S. Fileri (eds). Athens: Alexandreia.

Chordaki, E. (2020). Hidden Paths – Unconventional Practices: A Her-story of Circulation of the Medical Knowledge in the Late Twentieth Century. In G. N. Vlahakis and K. Tampakis, eds., *Science and Literature: Poetry and Prose*. National Hellenic Research Foundation (Digital Publication 08).

Chordaki, E. (2022). Science Communication in the Late 20th Century Greece: Public Intersections of Gender and Knowledge Circulation in the Feminist Birth Control Movements. PhD Thesis, Unpublished. Hellenic Open University.

Chordaki, E. (2022a). Science Communication Herstories: Reflecting on the Greek Feminist Birth Control Movement of the 1970s and 1980s. *Research for All*, 6(1), 1–8. https://doi.org/10.14324/RFA.06.1.13.

Chordaki, E. (2023). Ektrosi as Amvlosi and the Silent Procedure of Curettage for the Technical Termination of Pregnancy. *Feministiqa*, 6. https://feministiqa.net/ektrosi-os-amvlosi-siopili-diadikasia-apoksesis/ [Accessed March 30, 2024]. [In Greek].

Chordaki, E. (forthcoming a). The Valuable "s": Publics and Counterpublics of Abortion and Contraception in Greece in the Late 20th Century. Manuscript Accepted for Publication in the Edited Volume Women and Science in the 20th Century. Manchester: Manchester University Press.

Chordaki, E. (forthcoming b). The Collective and Historical Self: Vulnerable Epistemologies, Affective Politics, and Intergenerational Herstories. Manuscript Submitted for Publication in the Thematic Issue "Women's Movements and Formations of Knowledge – Political and Epistemic Practices" of *the Österreichische Zeitschrift für Geschichtswissenschaften (OeZG)*.

Chordaki, E. (2024). Experiential and Medical Expertise: Gender and Knowledge in the Greek Feminist Birth Control Movement, c. 1974–1986. In T. Loughran, H. Froom, K. Mahoney, and D. Payling, eds., *Embodiment, and Selfhood since 1950*. Manchester: Manchester University Press.

Chordaki, E. & Stavridi K. (2021). Neither Ba nor Bo. B@wie in the Feminist Space-Time. In A. Carastathis and B. Polykarpou, eds., *Come, Let Me Tell You: Feminist, Lesbian and Queer Narratives of the Post-Dictatorship Period*. Athens: FAC Press, pp. 55–66. (In Greek).

Collins, H. & Evans, R. (2002). The Third Wave of Science Studies: Studies of Expertise and Experience. *Social Studies of Science*, 32(2), 235–296.

Collins, H., & Evans, R. (2007). *Rethinking expertise*. University of Chicago Press.

Cresswelt, T. (1996). *In Place/Out of Place: Geography, Ideology, and Transgression*. Mineapolis: University of Minneapolis Press.

Crinon, N., Manes, C., Memmi, Aur. & Revault, C. (1979 [1978]). R. Papadopoulou (Trans.), M. Papadopoulou (Illustr.), *Clémentine ou la contraception*. Athens: Stohasmos. [Κλημεντίνη ή τα Αντισυλληπτικά].

CSHA: Women's Group of Law School, Female Nature: Anxieties and Paranoia. (Online collection). [Ομάδα Γυναικών Νομικής, Γυναικεία φύση: άγχη και παράνοια].

D'Agincourt-Canning, L. (2005). The Effect of Experiential Knowledge on Construction of Risk Perception in Hereditary Breast/Ovarian Cancer. *Journal of Genetic Counseling*, 14(1), 55–69.

Damianidi, A. (1986, May 20). Pro Life .... *Pantheon*. [Υπέρ της ζωής ... Πάνθεον].

Danezis, I. M. (1969). The Technical Abortion as an International and Greek Problem. *Medicine*, 15(3), 195–205 [Η τεχνητή έκτρωση ως διεθνές και ελληνικό πρόβλημα].

Davies, S. R., Halpern, M., Horst, M., Kirby, D. A., & Lewenstein, B. (2019). Science Stories as Culture: Experience, Identity, Narrative, and Emotion in Public Communication of Science. *JCOM*, 18(05). https://jcom.sissa.it/article/pubid/JCOM_1805_2019_A01/.

Davis, K. & Irvine J. (eds.) (2022). *Silences, Neglected Feelings and Blind-Spots in Research Practice*. Abingdon, Oxfordshire: Routledge.

DEC 1: Women's Liberation Movement: Sexuality and Contraception Group (1977). Contraception. (File 5–6–7–8 Sexuality/Reproductive Health).

DEC 2: Autonomous Women's Movement (1983, December). (File 7A. ΟΠΕ). [Αυτόνομη Κίνηση Γυναικών].

DEC 3: (1981, June 6–7). Third ISIS Conference (Women's International Information and Communication Service) on Women and Health, Held in Geneva. (File Health Issues).

Deutscher, P. (2017). *Foucault's Futures: A Critique of Reproductive Reason*. New York: Columbia University Press.

Dingli, S. & Cooke N. T. (eds.) (2019). *Political Silence: Meaning, Functions and Ambiguity*. Abingdon, Oxfordshire: Routledge.

Dixon, Th. (2011). Sensibility and History: The Importance of Lucien Febvre. *The History of Emotions Blog*. https://emotionsblog.history.qmul.ac.uk/2011/11/sensibility-and-history-the-importance-of-lucienfebvre/.

Drakopoulou, M. (1980, vol. 1). Unknown Title. *Sfynga*. [Σφίγγα].
Durbin, S. (2011). Creating Knowledge through Networks: A Gender Perspective. *Gender, Work and Organization*, 18(1), 90–122.
Editorial Board. (1979, vol. 1). Proceedings of the Discussion in the Parliament. Special Issue for Abortions. *Skoupa*. [Πρακτικά της Βουλής ή ευχαριστούμε, ώ Αντιπολίτευση, που αγωνίστηκες για να μας βλέπει μόνο ένας ψυχίατρος και όχι δύο. Αφιέρωμα: έκτρωση. Σκούπα. Για το Γυναικείο Ζήτημα].
Eichhorn, K. (2013). *The Archival Turn in Feminism*. Philadelphia: Temple University Press.
Eleftheros Typos 1: Unknown Author (1983, December 16). "Abortion Is Woman's Right." *Eleftheros Typos*. [Η άμβλωση είναι δικαίωμα της γυναίκας. Ελεύθερος Τύπος].
Eleftheros Typos 2: Unknown Author (1986, June 3). Significant Fight about Abortions. *Eleftheros Typos*. [Σημαντική μάχη για τις αμβλώσεις. Ελεύθερος Τύπος].
Eleftherotypia 1: Unknown Author (1983, April 10). Contraceptive Injection for Men. *Eleftherotypia*. [Αντισυλληπτική ένεση για τον Άνδρα. Ελευθεροτυπία].
Eleftherotypia 2: Unknown Author (1984, March 11). Contraception in the ... Hand. *Eleftherotypia*. [Αντισύλληψη στο ... μπράτσο. Ελευθεροτυπία].
Eleftherotypia 3: Unknown Author (1984, February 8). Autonomous Women: Free of Charge Abortions for all Women. *Eleftherotypia*. [Αυτόνομες: δωρεάν οι εκτρώσεις και για τις ανασφάλιστες. Ελευθεροτυπία].
Eleftherotypia 4: Unknown Author (1985, December 23). Family Planning. *Eleftherotypia*. [Οικογενειακός προγραμματισμός. Ελευθεροτυπία].
Ethnos 1: Unknown Author (1987, October 19). Quit the Pill Immediately. *Ethnos*. [Κόψτε αμέσως το χάπι. Έθνος].
Ethnos 2: Unknown Author (1986, April 2). War Fronts for Abortions. *Ethnos*. [Μέτωπο για τις αμβλώσεις. Έθνος].
Ethnos 3: Unknown Author (1986, April 28). We Are Perishing. *Ethnos*. [Χανόμαστε ... Έθνος].
Farakos, O. (1985, March 5). PASOK wants Greece to be a country of older people. *To Vima*. [Το ΠΑΣΟΚ μας θέλει χώρα γερόντων. Το Βήμα].
Felski, R. (2002). Telling Time in Feminist Theory. *Tulsa Studies in Women's Literature*, 21(1), 21–28.
Ferre, M. M., Gamson, W. A., Gerhards, J., and Rucht, D. (2002). Four Models of the Public Sphere in Modern Democracies. *Theory and Society*, 31, 289–324.
Fisher, P. (2007). Experiential Knowledge Challenges "Normality" and Individualized Citizenship: Towards "Another Way of Being." *Disability & Society*, 22(3), 283–298.

Flinterman, J. F., Teclemariam – Mesbah, R., Broerse, J. E. W., & Bunders, J. F. G. (2001). Transdisciplinarity: The New Challenge for Biomedical Research. *Bulletin of Science Technology & Society*, 21(4), 253–66.

Foster, H. (2004). An Archival Impulse. *October*, 110, 3–22.

Fraser, N. (1995). Politics, Culture, and the Public Sphere: Toward a Postmodern Conception. In L. Nicholson and S. Seidman, eds., *Social Postmodernism: Beyond Identity Politics*, 287–312. Cambridge: Cambridge University Press.

Freeman, E. (2010). *Time Binds: Queer Temporalities, Queer Histories.* Durham: Duke University Press.

Gaia: Unknown Author (1983). Women's Liberation and Class Struggle. *Gaia*. [Γυναικεία Απελευθέρωση και Ταξική Πάλη. Γαία].

Geoff, E. (2002). Politics, Culture and the Public Sphere. *Positions*, 10(1), 219–236.

GIK: Unknown Author (1984). Contraception or the Right to Control Ourselves, Our Body, and Our Lives. *Periodiko Omadas Paremvasis Koufalion*. [Αντισύλληψη ή το δικαίωμα να ελέγχουμε οι ίδιοι το σώμα και τη ζωή μας. Περιοδικό Ομάδας Παρέμβασης Κουφαλίων].

Greek Society of Family Planning (un.d.). *The Problem of Abortions in Today's Society.*[*Το πρόβλημα των αμβλώσεων στην σημερινή κοινωνία. Ελληνική Εταιρεία Οικογενειακού Προγραμματισμού*].

Gynaika: Unknown Author (1982, February). A Much Less Sexual Choice. *Gynaika*. [Μια ελάχιστα ερωτική επιλογή. Γυναίκα].

Halberstam, J. (1998). *Female Masculinity*. Durham: Duke University Press.

Halberstam, J. (2005). *In a Queer Time and Place: Transgender Bodies, Subcultural Lives*. New York: New York University Press.

Halpern, M. (2019). Feminist Standpoint Theory and Science Communication. *JCOM*, 18 (04), C02. https://doi.org/10.22323/2.18040302.

Haraway, D. (1988). Situated Knowledges: The Science Question in Feminism and the Privilege of Partial Perspective. *Feminist Studies*, 14(3), 575–99.

Hawkesworth, M. (2006). Gender and the Public: A Theoretical Overview. Prepared for Presentation at the 20th Congress of the International Political Science Association July 9–13.

Hesford, V. (2013). *Feeling Women's Liberation*. Durham: Duke University Press.

Hestia: Unknown Author (1986, February 26). They Condemn the Decriminalization of Abortions. *Hestia*. [Καταδικάζουν την αποποινικοποίηση των εκτρώσεων. Εστία].

Hilgartner, S. (1990). The Dominant View of Popularization: Conceptual Problems, Political Uses. *Social Studies of Science*, 20(3), 519–39.

Hooks, B. (1989). *Talking Back: Thinking Feminist, Thinking Black*. Abingdon, Oxfordshire: Routledge.

Hudson, N. (2018). Gender and the State. *Oxford Research Encyclopedia of International Studies*.

I Poli ton Gynaikon: Unknown Author (un.d.). Unknown Title. *I Poli ton Gynaikon*. [Πόλη των γυναικών].

Inhorn, M. C. & Whittle, K. L. (2001). Feminism Meets the "New" Epidemiologies: Toward an Appraisal of Antifeminist Biases in Epidemiological Research on Women's Health. *Social Science & Medicine*, 53, 553–67.

Joffe, C., Weitz, T., & Stacey, C. (2004). Uneasy Allies: Pro-choice Physicians, Feminist Health Activists and the Struggle for Abortion Rights. *Sociology of Health & Illness*, 26, 775–96.

Jones, R. D., Robinson, P. J., & Turner, J. (eds.) (2015). *The Politics of Hiding, Invisibility and Silence: Between Absence and Presence*. Abingdon, Oxfordshire: Routledge.

Julian, R., de Guevara Bliesemann, B., & Redhead, R. (2019). From Expert to Experiential Knowledge: Exploring the Inclusion of Local Experiences in Understanding Violence in Conflict. *Peacebuilding*, 1–16.

Karamanolakis, V. & Karpozilos, K. (2017). Ενότητα: Κοινωνία και Κινήματα. Project: *Δημιουργία ιστοσελίδας για την ιστορία της Μεταπολίτευσης 1974–1989*. Contemporary Social History Archives. http://metapolitefsi.com/%CE%95%CE%BD%CF%8C%CF%84%CE%B7%CF%84%CE%B5%CF%82/%CE%9A%CE%BF%CE%B9%CE%BD%CF%89%CE%BD%CE%AF%CE%B1.

Katina 14: Unknown Author (un.d., vol. 7). Sottosorpa. More Women than Men. *Katina*. [Sottosorpa. Περισσότερες γυναίκες από ότι άνδρες ... Κατίνα].

Katina 2: Unknown Author (1988, vol. 3). An Androcentric and Technocratic Symposium, or What Else Could It Be or What Else Could Not Be. *Katina*. [Συμπόσιο ανδροκρατικό και τεχνοκρατικό ή τί άλλο μπορούσε να είναι η να μην ήταν καθόλου. Κατίνα].

Katina 3: Unknown Author (1987, vol. 2). A Feminist Coalition. *Katina*. [Γυναικεία συμμαχία ή τι γυρεύει η αλεπού στο παζάρι. Κατίνα].

Kazakopoulou, K. & Papastathopoulou, C. (1984, January 21). Abortions: Yes, for all Ages. *Eleftherotypia*. [Αμβλώσεις: ναι από όλες τις ηλικίες. Ελευθεροτυπία].

Kefala, P. (1984, March). File . . . Abortions. *Bourda*. [Φάκελος . . . εκτρώσεις. Μπούρντα].

Kennedy, H. (2015). "Rethinking Expertise," *The Journal of Forensic Psychiatry & Psychology*, 20(4), 613–16.

Kiveli (1979, vol. 1). "Poem of Kiveli. Special Issue for abortions," *Skoupa*. [Ποίημα. Αφιέρωμα: έκτρωση. Σκούπα. Για το Γυναικείο Ζήτημα].

Kostis, K. (2018). *Τα κακομαθημένα παιδιά της ιστορίας. Η διαμόρφωση του νεοελληνικού κράτους $18^{ος}$-$21^{ος}$ αιώνας*.Athens: Patakis.

Kotsovelou, V. & Repousi, M. (1989, vol. 4). Thoughts for the Political Identity of Feminism in Greece. *Dini*. [Σκέψεις για την πολιτική ταυτότητα του φεμινισμού στην Ελλάδα. Δίνη].

Kourkoula, Ch. (1983, vol. 19). Sexual Revolution. Sexual Liberation. *O Agonas tis Gynaikas*. [Σεξουαλική επανάσταση. Σεξουαλική απελευθέρωση. Ο Αγώνας της Γυναίκας].

Kyriakatiki Eleftherotypia 7: Unknown Author (1981, August 16). What does the Greek woman know about contraception. *Kyriakatiki Eleftherotypia*. [Τι γνωρίζει η ελληνίδα για την αντισύλληψη. Κυριακάτικη Ελευθεροτυπία].

Kyriakatiki Eleftherotypia 7: Unknown Author (1984, April 1). The Dangers. *Kyriakatiki Eleftherotypia*. [Οι κίνδυνοι. Κυριακάτικη Ελευθεροτυπία].

Lässig, S. (2016). The History of Knowledge and the Expansion of the Historical Research Agenda. *Bulletin of the GHI Washington*, 59, 29–58.

Lee A. J. (2017). A Queer/ed Archival Methodology: Archival Bodies as Nomadic Subjects. *Critical Archival Studies*, 1(2), 1–27.

Lewenstein, B. (2019). The Need for Feminist Approaches to Science Communication. *JCOM*, 18(04). https://doi.org/10.22323/2.18040301.

LHP 1: Penal Code (1835). [Ποινικός Νόμος του Βασιλείου της Ελλάδας]. http://srv1-vivl-volou.mag.sch.gr/islandora/object/voDKI%3A223.

LHP 2: Meeting ΞΕ' July 26, 1950; 65th Meeting July 26; 1950, 66th Meeting July 27; 1950. [Συνεδριάσεις στην Βουλή].

LHP 3: Meeting PM' Monday May 26, 1986 [Συνεδρίαση στην Βουλή].

LHP 4: Meeting PMB' Wednesday May 28, 1986 [Συνεδρίαση στην Βουλή].

LHP 5: Meeting PME' Monday June 2, 1986 [Συνεδρίαση στην Βουλή].

LHP 6: Meeting PMZ' Wednesday June 4, 1986 [Συνεδρίαση στην Βουλή].

LHP 7: Meeting PMH' Thursday June 5, 1986 [Συνεδρίαση στην Βουλή].

LHP 8: Meeting PNT' Thursday June 12, 1986 [Συνεδρίαση στην Βουλή].

LHP 9: Meeting PNΓ' Wednesday June 12, 1986 [Συνεδρίαση στην Βουλή].

LHP 10: Explanatory Report for the Law "For the Information of Intended Spouses and Married Couples Regarding Genetics and Family Planning Issues." Ath. Kanelopoulos (Minister of Economics), Sp. Doxiadis (Minister of Social Services), August 6, 1979. [Εισηγητική Έκθεση].

LHP 11: Law 1492/1950. For the Constitutional Validity of the Greek Penal Code. [Περί κυρώσεως του Ποινικού Κώδικα].
LHP 12: Law 821/1978. For the Removal or Transplant of Human Biological Substances. [Περί αφαιρέσεων και μεταμοσχεύσεων βιολογικών ουσιών ανθρώπινης προελεύσεως].
LHP 13: Law 1609/1986. Technical Termination of Pregnancy and Protection of Women's Health and Other Regulations. [Τεχνητή διακοπή της εγκυμοσύνης και προστασία της γυναίκας και άλλες διατάξεις].
LHP 14: Law 1492/1950. For the Constitutional Validity of the Greek Penal Code. [Περί κυρώσεως του Ποινικού Κώδικα].
Liakos, A. (2022). *Ο ελληνικός 20^{ος} αιώνας*. 3rd ed. Athens: Polis.
Louros, K. N. (1976). Savers and Hangmen with Dresses. *Eleftho*, 6. [Σωτήρες και Δήμιοι με φουστάνια. Ελευθώ].
Louis, E. (2018). *Who Killed My Father*. New York: Penguin Random House.
Louis, E. (2022). *A Woman's Battles and Transformations*. New York: Penguin Random House.
Mahairopoulou, M. (1982, October 20). Contraception: An Interesting Discussion with the Gynecologost N. Manouilidis. *Woman*. [Η αντισύλληψη. Μια ενδιαφέρουσα συζήτηση με τον γυναικολόγο κ. Νικόλαο Μανουηλίδι. Γυναίκα].
Manidaki, A. (2020). The History of Family Planning in Greece. Dissertation. The University of Crete. School of Health Science. Department of Medicine (in Greek). [Η ιστορία του οικογενειακού προγραμματισμού στην Ελλάδα].
Marshall, D. & Tortorici, Z. (eds.) (2022). *Turning Archival: The Life of the Historical in Queer Studies*. Durham: Duke University Press.
Mazur, A. G. & McBride, D. E. (2007). State Feminism since the 1980s: From Loose Notion to Operationalized Concept. *Politics & Gender*, 3(4), 501–13.
Mazur, A. G. & McBride, D. E. (2008). State Feminism. In Z. Goertz and A. G. Mazur, eds., *Politics, Gender, and Concepts: Theory and Methodology*. Cambridge: Cambridge University Press, pp. 244–69.
McCormick, S., Brown, P., & Zavestoski, S. (2003). The Personal Is Scientific, the Scientific Is Political: The Public Paradigm of the Environmental Breast Cancer Movement. *Sociological Forum*, 18(4), 545–76.
Medusa 1: Unknown Author. (1983, vol. 1). Abortions and Contraception. A Retrospect. *Medusa*. [Εκτρώσεις αντισύλληψη. Ιστορική αναδρομή. Μέδουσα].
Medusa 2: Unknown Author (1983, vol. 1). Sexuality and Women's Discourse. *Medusa*. [Σεξουαλικότητα και γυναικείος λόγος Μέδουσα].
Mesimvrini 1: Unknown Author (1983, December 10). Women Are the Victims. *Mesimvrini*. [Θύματα οι γυναίκες. Μεσημβρινή].

Mesimvrini 2: Unknown Author (1986, May 14). Psaroudakis Attacks to Margaret. *Mesimvrini*. [Επίθεση ψαρουδάκη κατά της μάργκαρετ. Μεσημβρινή].

Metropolitan Timotheos. (1985, February 17). I Follow the Arguments. *Thesmos*. ['Εθνος].

Meulenbelt, A. (1984 [1981]). *For Ourselves*. A. A. Verikokaki (Transl.) Our Bodies and Sexuality from Women's Point of View. Athens: Nea Sinora, A. A. Livani. [Για μας τις γυναίκες].

Mpenou, L. (1985, October). Occasioned by the Abortion Bill. *Fylladio*. [Μ' αφορμή το νομοσχέδιο για τις εκτρώσεις. Φυλλάδιο].

Mpredakis, M. (1986, April 18). A Gynecologist Close to Women: Contraceptive Methods. *Ntomino*. [Ο γυναικολόγος κοντά σας/ μέθοδοι αντισύλληψης. Ντόμινο].

Movement for the Liberation of Women. (1977). *Methods of Contraception*. Movement for the Liberation of Women. [Κίνηση για την Απελευθέρωση των Γυναικών. Αντισυλληπτικά Μέσα].

Negt, O., Kluge, A., & Labanyi, P. (trasnl.) (1988). The Public Sphere and Experience: Selections. *October*, 46, 60–82.

Nijs, G. & Heylinghen, A. (2015). Turning Disability into Expertise in Assessing Building Accessibility: A Contribution to Articulating Disability Epistemology. *ALTER European Journal of Disability Research*, 9, 144–56.

Nimkulrat, N., Groth, C., Tomico, O., & Valle-Noronha, J. (2020). Knowing together-Experiential Knowledge and Collaboration. *International Journal of CoCreation in Design and the Arts*, 16(4), 267–73.

Oi Filoi ton Polyteknon 1: Unknown Author (1983, March). Study-Research. Towards the Decriminalization of Abortions?!. *Oi Filoi ton Polyteknon*. [Μελέτη -έρευνα/ Προς νομιμοποίηση των εκτρώσεων ;! Οι φίλοι των πολυτέκνων].

Oi Filoi ton Polyteknon 2: Unknown Author (1983, March). Study-Research. Towards the Decriminalization of Abortions?!. *Oi Filoi ton Polyteknon*. [Μελέτη -έρευνα/ Προς νομιμοποίηση των εκτρώσεων ;! Οι φίλοι των πολυτέκνων].

Oi Filoi ton Polyteknon 3: Unknown Author (1985). A Specialized Committee Studies the Problem of Abortions – in the End Abortions Are Being Decriminalized. *Oi Filoi ton Polyteknon* [Ειδική επιτροπή μελετά το πρόβλημα των αμβλώσεων – τελικά οι αμβλωσεις νομιμοποιούνται. Οι φίλοι των πολυτέκνων].

Oikogeneia: Unknown Author (1985). Rare Visualization of the Holly Conception with Soul and Body from the Moment of Conception. *Oikogeneia*. [Σπάνια απεικόνιση -δογματική της θείας συλλήψεως – ενανθρωπήσεως του Θεού Λόγου ως θεανθρώπου Χριστού με πρόσληψη ψυχής και σώματος εξ άκρας συλλήψεως. Οικογένεια].

Östling, J., Sandmo, E., Larsson Heidenblad, D., Nilsson Hammar, A., & Nordberg, K. (eds.) (2018). *Circulation of Knowledge: Explorations in the History of Knowledge.* Lund: Nordic Academic Press.

PACL 1: Declaration. Autonomous Women's Movement (1983, April). Campaign for the Right to Abortion, Contraception, Sexuality. [Προκήρυξη Αυτόνομης Κίνησης Γυναικών για την Καμπάνια για το δικαίωμα στην έκτρωση, αντισύλληψη και σεξουαλικότητα].

PACL 2: Women's House of Kesariani. (1983). Contraception and Women's Emancipation. [Σπίτι Γυναικών Καισαριανής. Αντισύλληψη και γυναικεία χειραφέτηση].

PACL 3: Public Statement of Women Who Had Aborted. (1983, April). [Δημόσια δήλωση γυναικών που έχουν κάνει έκτρωση].

PACL 4: Women's Global Network for Reproductive Rights. (1986, June). Reproductive Rights International Tribunal. Divided in Culture United in Struggle.

PACL 17: Women's House of Kesariani. Contraception and Women's Emancipation. [Σπίτι Γυναικών Καισαριανής. Αντισύλληψη και γυναικεία χειραφέτηση.

Pajnik, M. (2006). Feminist Reflections on Habermas's Communicative Action: The Need for an Inclusive Political Theory. *European Journal of Social Theory*, 9(3), 385–404.

Pambouki, E. (1979). Republication: Children's Books about Sex Education. *Skoupa*, 3. [Από τα παιδικά βιβλία της σεξουαλικής αγωγής. Σκούπα].

Panhellenic Medical Association (1983, November). Decriminalization of abortions. *Iatriko Vima*. [Η αποποινικοποίηση των εκτρώσεων. Ιατρικό Βήμα].

Pantheon 1: Unknown Author (1981, November 10). Adolescence and Contraceptive Methods in France. *Pantheon*. [Εφηβεία και αντισυλληπτικές μέθοδοι στην Γαλλία. Πάνθεον].

Pantheon 2: Unknown Author (1986, February). The First Steps. *Pantheon*. [Πρώτα βήματα!. Πάνθεον].

Pantheon 3: Unknown Author (1984, January 1). Under Conditions. *Pantheon*. [Υπό όρους. Πάνθεον].

Papadogianis, N. (2015). Νεανική πολιτικοποίηση και «πολιτισμός» στα πρώτα χρόνια της Μεταπολίτευσης. In M. Avgeridis, E. Gazi, & K. Kornetis, eds., *Μεταπολίτευση. Η Ελλάδα στο μεταίχμιο των δύο αιώνων*. Athens: Themelio, pp. 133–50.

Papanikolaou, D. (2018). Archive Trouble. In P. Petsini, ed., *Capitalist Realism. Future Perfect / Past Continuous*. Thessaloniki: University of Macedonia Press, pp. 162–73.

Papanikolaou, N. A. (1986). *Gynecology*. 2nd ed. Thessaloniki. [Γυναικολογία].

Papanikolaou, N. A. (1987). *Obstetrics*. 2nd ed. Thessaloniki [Μαιευτική].

Papanikolaou, N. A. (1987a). *Surgeries in Gynecology and Obstetrics*. Thessaloniki [Επεμβάσεις στην γυναικολογία και την μαιευτική].

Papastathopoulou, Chr. (1983a, December 9). "1390 Doctors Share 4,5 Billion from Abortions. Women's Campagn for the Right to Abortion-Contraception-Sexuality." *Eleftherotypia*. [1390 γιατροί μοιράζονται 4,5 δισ. από τις αμβλώσεις [Εκστρατεία γυναικών για δικαίωμα σε έκτρωση – αντισύλληψη – σεξουαλικότητα. Ελευθεροτυπία].

Pavlopoulos, S. & Fitili, M. (2017). Μεταπολίτευση: από την στιγμή στην διάρκεια. Τα χρόνια 1974–1989. Project: *Δημιουργία ιστοσελίδας για την ιστορία της Μεταπολίτευσης 1974–1989*. Contemporary Social History Archives. http://metapolitefsi.com/%CE%A4%CE%B1%CF%85%CF%84%CF%8C%CF%84%CE%B7%CF%84%CE%B1.

Preveroudakis, K., Soumplis, A., & Papathanasiou, Z. (1980). Current Issues in Obstetrics and Gynecology. Vol. II. Kovanis H., Preveroudakis K., Soumplis A., Papathanasiou Z. Athens. [Επίκαιρα θέματα Γυναικολογίας και Μαιευτικής].

Puwar, N. (2004). *Space Invaders: Race, Gender and Bodies out of Place*. Berg.

Rai, S., ed. (2003). *Mainstreaming Gender, Democratizing the State? Institutional Mechanisms for the Advancement of Women*. Manchester: Manchester University Press.

Rapitou, A. (1981, vol. 12). Women's Rights Have Tested by the European Parliament. *Anichto Parathyro*. [Τα δικαιώματα της γυναίκας δοκιμάστηκαν σκληρά από το Ευρωπαϊκό Κοινοβούλιο. Ανοιχτό Παράθυρο].

Reddy, W. M. (2000). Sentimentalism and Its Erasure: The Role of Emotions in the Era of the French Revolution. *Journal of Modern History*, 72, 109–52.

Rice, L. J., Burke, J. B., & Heynen, N. (2015). Knowing Climate Change, Embodying Climate Praxis: Experiential Knowledge in Southern Appalachia. *Annals of the Association of American Geographers*, 105(2), 253–62.

Rixi 1: Unknown Author (1984, February). The Decriminalization and the Preventative Reformism of PASOK. *Rixi*. [Νομιμοποίηση της έκτρωσης και προληπτικός ρεφορμισμός του ΠΑΣΟΚ. Ρήξη].

Rixi 2: Unknown Author (1983, August). Autonomous Women's Movement's Declaration. Campaign: The Right to Abortion-Contraception-Sexuality. *Rixi*. [Διακήρυξη Αυτόνομη Κίνηση Γυναικών Καμπάνια: Δικαίωμα στην έκτρωση αντισύλληψη- σεξουαλικότητα. Ρήξη].

Rizas, S. (2017). Ενότητα: Ευρώπη. Project: *Δημιουργία ιστοσελίδας για την ιστορία της Μεταπολίτευσης 1974–1989*. Contemporary Social History Archives. http://metapolitefsi.com/%CE%95%CE%BD%CF%8C%CF%84%CE%B7%CF%84%CE%B5%CF%82/%CE%95%CF%85%CF%81%CF%8E%CF%80%CE%B7.

Rosenwein, B., & Riccardo, C. (2018). *What Is the History of Emotions?* Cambridge: Polity.

Samiou, D. (2012). So Difficult to be Considered as Citizens: The History of Women's Suffrage in Greece, 1864–2001. In B. Rodriguez Ruiz and R. Rubio Marin, eds., *The Struggle for Female Suffrage in Europe*. Leiden: Brill, pp. 439–51.

Samiou, D. (2013). *Τα πολιτικά δικαιώματα των Ελληνίδων 1864–1952. Ιδιότητα του πολίτη και καθολική ψηφοφορία*. Athens: P. N. Sakoulas / Law and Economics.

Sedgwick, K. E. (1997). Paranoid Reading and Reparative Reading; or, You Are so Paranoid, You Probably Think This Introduction Is about You. In E. K. Sedgwick, ed., *Novel Gazing: Queer Readings in Fiction*. Durham: Duke University Press, pp. 1–38.

Serdedakis, N. (2015). Συνέχειες και ασυνέχειες της συλλογικής δράσης κατά την μετάβαση από την «καχεκτική δημοκρατία» στη Μεταπολίτευση. In M. Avgeridis, E. Gazi, K. Kornetis, eds., *Μεταπολίτευση. Η Ελλάδα στο μεταίχμιο των δύο αιώνων*. Athens: Themelio, pp. 99–115.

Doe, J. (1989). *Sex Education: Gender Relations and What Young People Should Know* (2nd ed.). Athens.

Sfynga: Unknown Author (1980, vol. 1). A Small Group. *Sfynga*. [Μικρή ομάδα. Σφίγγα].

Stewart, K. (2008). Weak Theory in an Unfinished World. *Journal of Folklore Research*, 45(1), 71–82.

Susen, S. (2011). Critical Notes on Habermas's Theory of the Public Sphere. *Sociological Analysis*, 5(1), 37–62.

Sygchroni Gynaika 60: Unknown Author (1985, vol. 41). The Greek Council for Equality. Three Years since Its Foundation. A Conversation with Chr. Laiou. *Sygchroni Gynaika*. [Συμβούλιο Ισότητας. Τρία χρόνια ύπαρξης. Πως αξιολογούνται; Μια συζήτηση με την κα. Χρ. Λαΐου. Σύγχρονη Γυναίκα].

Ta Nea 1: Unknown Author (1983, April 6). Unknown Title. *Ta Nea*. [Τα Νέα].

Ta Nea 2: Unknown Author (1976, January 28). The Government Remains Silent, the Political Parties Discuss and the Doctors Stagnate. However, Death Rates Are Rising, Part III. *Ta Nea*. [Η κυβέρνηση παραμένει σιωπηλή, τα κόμματα συζητούν και οι γιατροί αδιαφορούν. Ωστόσο, οι αριθμοί θανάτων αυξάνονται. Τα Νέα].

Ta Nea 3: Unknown Author (1984, February 2). The Church's Opinion. *Ta Nea*. [Η άποψη της Εκκλησίας. Τα Νέα].

Theofilos from Gortinia and Megalopoli (1986, April 28). Again Abortions. *Eleftherotypia*. [Ξανά οι αμβλώσεις. Ελευθεροτυπία].

Theoharatos, Chr. (1985, November 24). The Solution of the Demographic Is the Third Child. *Ethnos*. [Τρίτο παιδί η λύση του δημογραφικού. Έθνος].

Thourios: Unknown Author (1981, March 12). Another Aspect: The Church Regarding Abortions. *Thourios*. [Η άλλη όψη του νομίσματος: Η άποψη της Εκκλησίας. Θούριος].

Topham, J. R. (2009). Introduction. *Isis*, 100(2), 310–18.

To Vima 1: Unknown Author (1984, March 25). Contraceptive Sponge. *To Vima*. [Και αντισυλληπτικό σπόγγος. Το Βήμα].

To Vima 2: Unknown Author (1985, May 19). The Pill Is 25 Years Old. *To Vima*. [Το χάπι έγινε εικοσι πέντε χρονών. Το Βήμα].

To Vima 3: Unknown Author (1985, January 23). Pro-choice Supporters Are Terrified. *To Vima*. [Τρομοκρατούνται οι υπέρμαχοι των αμβλώσεων. Το Βήμα].

To Vima 4: Unknown Author (1986, February 2). Discussions in the Newspaper. Yes or No to Abortions. Experts Discuss. *To Vima*. [Διάλογοι του Βήματος/ Ναι ή όχι στις αμβλώσεις. Το Βήμα].

To Vima 5: Unknown Author (1985, December 1). The Reason behind Miscarriages Is … OB/GYN Pr. Komninos A. Discusses the Issue. *To Vima*. [Αιτία των πολλών αποβολών η … πρόεδρος της ιατρικής/ Ο καθηγητής Μαιευτικής και γυναικολογίας του Παν/μου Αθηνών κ. Αντώνης Κομνηνός ομιλεί για τις αποβολές. Το Βήμα].

To Vima 6: Unknown Author (1985, March 5). The Greeks Become Less. *To Vima*. [Λιγοστεύουμε οι Έλληνες. Το Βήμα].

Valasi, D. (1985, December 13). While the Church Disapproves, Women Claim Their Right for Free Abortions. *Macedonia*. [Ενώ η εκκλησία αποδοκιμάζει οι γυναίκες διεκδικούν το δικαίωμα ελεύθερων αμβλώσεων. Μακεδονία].

Varika, E. (2011 [1986]). *Η εξέγερση των κυριών. Η γένεση μιας φεμινιστικής συνείδησης στην Ελλάδα 1833–1907*. Athens: Papazisis.

Vassili, M. (2022). *Η άμβλωση ως δικαίωμα: λόγοι και αντίλογοι γύρω από ένα φεμινιστικό πρόταγμα (1976–1986)*. Unpublished Master Thesis. Crete: University of Crete.

Vieira, B. M. (2020). The Great Wall of Silence: Voice-Silence Dynamics in Authoritarian Regimes. *Critical Review of International Social and Political Philosophy*, 368–91.

Vieira, B. M. (2020a). Representing Silence in Politics. *American Political Science Review*, 114(4), 976–88.

Vieira, B. M., Jung, T., Gray, S., & Rollo, T. (2019). The Nature of Silence and its Democratic Possibilities. *Contemporary Political Theory*, 18, 424–47.
Vita, A. (1976). In the Aftermath of the Year of the Woman. *Eleftho*, 1. [Ο απόηχος του έτους της γυναίκας. Ελευθώ].
Vradini 1: Unknown Author (1986, January 26). Representatives of the National Organization of Multi-Child Parents Stand against Abortions. *Vradini*. [Οχι στις αμβλώσεις Εκπρόσωποι της εθνικής οργάνωσης πολυτέκνων. Βραδυνή].
Vradini 2: Unknown Author (1986, January 18). Six Indictments from the Priesthood. *Vradini*. [Έξι κατηγορώ από το ιερατείο. Βραδυνή].
Vradini 3: Unknown Author (1986, January 20). The Lawyer Ch. Salavrakou Discussed with us the Two Aspects, the Conflict between the State and the Church and the Legal Problem. *Vradini*. [Για τις δύο απόψεις και τη διαμάχη κράτους και εκκλησίας αλλά και για το νομικό πρόβλημα μας μίλησε η δικηγόρος κ Χρύσα Σαλαβράκου. Βραδυνή].
Warner, M. (2005). *Publics and Counterpublics*. New York: Zone Books.
Women's Collective, & Malliakou, Nt. (1981, vol. 1). For the Creation of Women's Groups of Self-consciousness. *I Poli ton Gynaikon*. [Για την δημιουργία των γυναικείων ομάδων αυτοσυνείδησης. [Πόλη των γυναικών].
Women's Collective, & Malliakou, Nt. (1982, vol. 2). For the creation of women's groups of self-consciousness. *I Poli ton Gynaikon*. [Για την δημιουργία των γυναικείων ομάδων αυτοσυνείδησης. [Πόλη των γυναικών].
Women's Group in Denmark. (1980 [1975].). *Woman and Her Body*. Translated by M. Parashis and edited by Dr. Alekou, Athens: Odisseas [(Kvinde kend din krop). Ομάδα Γυναικών Δανίας. Η γυναίκα και το κορμί της].
Wynne, B. & Lynch, M. (2015). Science and Technology Studies: Experts and Expertise. *Political Science. Technology & Society*, 21(4), 253–66.
Xiridaki, K. (2020). *Το φεμινιστικό κίνημα στην Ελλάδα 1830–1936*. Πρωτοπόρες Γυναίκες [Feminist Movements in Greece 1830–1936: Pioneering Women]. Athens: Koukida.
Young, I. M. (1990). Five Faces of Oppression. In I. M. Young, ed., *Justice and the Politics of Difference*. Princeton: Princeton University Press, pp. 39–65.

Cambridge Elements

Histories of Emotions and the Senses

Series Editors
Rob Boddice
Tampere University

Rob Boddice (PhD, FRHistS) is Senior Research Fellow at the Academy of Finland Centre of Excellence in the History of Experiences. He is the author/editor of thirteen books, including *Knowing Pain: A History of Sensation, Emotion and Experience* (Polity Press, 2023); *Humane Professions: The Defence of Experimental Medicine, 1876–1914* (Cambridge University Press, 2021) and *A History of Feelings* (Reaktion, 2019).

Piroska Nagy
Université du Québec à Montréal (UQAM)

Piroska Nagy is Professor of Medieval History at the Université du Québec à Montréal (UQAM) and initiated the first research program in French on the history of emotions. She is the author or editor of fourteen volumes, including *Le Don des larmes au Moyen Âge* (Albin Michel, 2000); *Medieval Sensibilities: A History of Emotions in the Middle Ages*, with Damien Boquet (Polity, 2018); and *Histoire des émotions collectives: Épistémologie, émergences*, expériences, with D. Boquet and L. Zanetti Domingues (Classiques Garnier, 2022).

Mark Smith
University of South Carolina

Mark Smith (PhD, FRHistS) is Carolina Distinguished Professor of History and Director of the Institute for Southern Studies at the University of South Carolina. He is author or editor of over a dozen books and his work has been translated into Chinese, Korean, Danish, German, and Spanish. He has lectured in Europe, throughout the United States, Australia, and China and his work has been featured in the New York Times, the London Times, the Washington Post, and the Wall Street Journal. He serves on the US Commission for Civil Rights.

About the Series
Born of the emotional and sensory "turns", Elements in Histories of Emotions and the Senses move one of the fastest-growing interdisciplinary fields forward. The series is aimed at scholars across the humanities, social sciences, and life sciences, embracing insights from a diverse range of disciplines, from neuroscience to art history and economics. Chronologically and regionally broad, encompassing global, transnational, and deep history, it concerns such topics as affect theory, intersensoriality, embodiment, human–animal relations, and distributed cognition. The founding editor of the series was Jan Plamper.

Cambridge Elements

Histories of Emotions and the Senses

Elements in the Series

Sensory Perception, History and Geology: The Afterlife of Molyneux's Question in British, American and Australian Landscape Painting and Cultural Thought
Richard Read

Love in Contemporary Technoculture
Ania Malinowska

Memes, History and Emotional Life
Katie Barclay and Leanne Downing

Boredom
Elena Carrera

Marketing Violence: The Affective Economy of Violent Imageries in the Dutch Republic
Frans-Willem Korsten, Inger Leemans, Cornelis van der Haven and Karel Vanhaesebrouck

Beyond Compassion: Gender and Humanitarian Action
Dolores Martín-Moruno

Uncertainty and Emotion in the 1900 Sydney Plague
Philippa Nicole Barr

Sensorium: Contextualizing the Senses and Cognition in History and Across Cultures
David Howes

Zionism: Emotions, Language, and Experience
Ofer Idels

Affective Touching: Neurobiology and Technological Applications
Mark Paterson

Embodied Epistemology as Rigorous Historical Method
Lauren Mancia

Making Sense of Knowledge: Feminist Epistemologies in the Greek Birth Control Movement (1974–1986)
Evangelia (Lina) Chordaki

A full series listing is available at: www.cambridge.org/HOES

Printed by Integrated Books International,
United States of America

About **Sino**ist Books

We hope you enjoyed this exciting story of Feng Meng'ao's quest for peace.

SINOIST BOOKS brings the best of Chinese fiction to English-speaking readers. We aim to create a greater understanding of Chinese culture and society, and provide an outlet for the ideas and creativity of the country's most talented authors.

To let us know what you thought of this book, or to learn more about the diverse range of exciting Chinese fiction in translation we publish, find us online. If you're as passionate about Chinese literature as we are, then we'd love to hear your thoughts!

sinoistbooks.com
@sinoistbooks